Food Fest!

Your Complete Guide to Florida's Food Festivals

Joan Steinbacher

Bee Cliff Press
Seminole, FL

Copyright © 2007 Joan Steinbacher. All rights reserved. No part of this book may be reproduced or transmitted in any form or by any means, electronic or mechanical, including photocopying, recording, or by an information storage and retrieval system—except by a reviewer who may quote brief passages in a review to be printed in a magazine, newspaper, or on the Web—without permission in writing from the publisher.

Published by Bee Cliff Press, P.O. Box 8598, Seminole, FL 33775; info@BeeCliffPress.com; (800) 930-4731.

Notice: Although the author and publisher have made every effort to ensure the accuracy and completeness of information contained in this book, we assume no responsibility for errors, inaccuracies, omissions, or any inconsistency herein. Any slights of people, places, events, or organizations are unintentional.

Printed and bound in the United States of America.

Cover design by 1106 Design.

ISBN-13: 978-0-9779846-0-2
ISBN-10: 0-9779846-0-5

Library of Congress Control Number: 2006908102

ATTENTION CORPORATIONS, GOVERNMENT, AND PROFESSIONAL ORGANIZATIONS: Quantity discounts are available on bulk purchases of this book for educational, gift purposes, or as premiums for increasing membership or magazine and newspaper subscriptions and renewals. For information, please contact Bee Cliff Press, P.O. Box 8598, Seminole, FL 33775; info@BeeCliffPress.com; (800) 930-4731.

ACKNOWLEDGMENTS

Thanks to the many event organizers and Chambers of Commerce staff who contributed information and verified the details contained in this book.

Table of Contents

Chapter 1: Food, Glorious Food!   1
   Tips and Suggestions   3
   Book Organization and Event Listings   4
   How to Use the Companion Website   5

Chapter 2: Seafood Fiesta   7

Chapter 3: Carnivore's Delight   43

Chapter 4: Fruit Medley   83

Chapter 5: Vegan's Variety   99

Chapter 6: Drink, Drank, Drunk   107

Chapter 7: Miscellaneous Munchies   127

Chapter 8: Tantalizing Tastes   135

Appendix A: Directory by Region   149
   Map 1: Florida Regional Map   150
   Map 2: North Regions   151
   Map 3: Central Regions   154
   Map 4: South Regions   159

Appendix B: Directory by Month   163

Appendix C: Alphabetical Listing   173

Appendix D: Bonus Recipes   183

Index   187

1 Food, Glorious Food!

What better way for Floridians to show pride in our heritage, our towns, and the fruit of our fields or the catch of our rivers and oceans, than to host a food festival? These festivals have always been a means of uniting communities through celebrations of harvests and giving thanks for a plentiful growing season. They can be traced back thousands of years to celebrating the arrival of harvest time, the autumnal equinox, and the honoring of earth gods.

Combining the excitement of celebrations with the fresh taste of local foods, Florida's food festivals continue those traditions today—typically honoring a crop grown or seafood harvested in the region. From mullet to crawfish, frog legs to sausage, mangos to kumquats, garlic to swamp cabbage, flap jacks to chocolate, and anything and everything in between, there's a festival for every taste.

Florida's food festivals are ideal entertainment for the whole family. Besides the main attraction—delicious food—these festivals feature a variety of events. Education abounds at the "Garlic University" during Delray Beach's Garlic Fest. Country music fills the sprawling festival grounds in daily concerts at the Plant City Strawberry Festival. Eating contests are popular, as well as off-beat competitions such as the "pig chase" at the Jay Peanut Festival or the "Tickle Pig" contest at the Pig on the Pond where participants decorate

Heading to a kid's zone.

porta-potties. Like fairs or carnivals, food festivals often feature children's activities and exciting midways with their flashing lights, daredevil rides, and games of chance.

Playing on the midway.

Pageants are often highlighted by the crowning of the festival queen. Small or elaborate parades create fun for all ages with imaginative floats and marching bands. Races burn off calories—or build an appetite. Evenings are crowned with firework shows. Slower-paced attendees can meander through arts and craft booths, farmers markets, or displays of antique cars, fire engines, or farm equipment. For those strictly there for the food, many festivals hold recipe competitions or cookoffs.

Waving at a passing float.

The best thing about Florida's food festivals is that none of the rules your mother taught you apply. You can eat with your hands and put your elbows on the table, wipe your mouth on your sleeve, and lick your fingers before wiping them on your pants. It's no wonder people love food fests!

The Sunshine State is known internationally for its great food. The best places to find the heart and soul of tasty Florida fare is in the multitude of local food festivals held throughout the year in the state's pleasant and welcoming climate. So get outdoors and enjoy the clear air and sunshine.

Many festivals have a small-town character, while others have gained nationwide recognition. Festival length varies—from one-day affairs to a week or more.

While most Florida food festivals are free or charge a nominal admission fee, and many offer free samples, some are ticketed events for admission and/or the food. Depending on the location, there may be a parking charge. Since fees change frequently, please contact the festivals ahead of time so there are no surprises. Keep in mind that many festival proceeds go to charity, which may make swallowing the cost more palatable.

At most food festivals, you go from booth to booth (pay as you go) and sample different foods or recipes of the same food. But others have whole meals for purchase or are sit-down meals. Festivals may feature a particular raw ingredient (like strawberries or tomatoes) while others involve preparing dishes onsite (like chili or barbecue). Or if you crave variety, "Taste Of" events typically feature the signature dishes of local restaurants.

Bon appétit!

Tips and Suggestions

- Always consult the website, call, or e-mail to confirm the details of each festival before you set off. On occasion events get moved or cancelled. Though we've checked and double-checked, you should still verify dates and times. Find out what day and time special activities will be held. You don't want to travel even a short distance only to find the most interesting activity at the festival occurred a day or an hour before your arrival! Ask about admission fees—they often change year to year.
- Check the weather—always an important consideration while traveling. Bring rain gear, especially in the summer months when storms pop up without notice. If you're at an outdoor festival and hear thunder, take cover as soon as possible. Florida isn't called the Lightning Capital of the World for nothing. Fried food may be detrimental to your health, but fried you is downright hazardous.
- If you're bringing kids or a large group, consider taking walkie talkies. If you split up you can contact each other without paying for cell phone minutes. Besides, they're fun toys—even for grownups. Don't forget to decide on a frequency channel before going your separate ways.

- Bring the sun protection your dermatologist (and mother) always hound you about—sunscreen, hat, water. It's hot in Florida.
- Wet naps or hand sanitizers will help with grimy hands, especially on the car ride home. You don't want a sticky steering wheel.
- Take a lightweight tote to carry purchases and essentials—like this book!

Book Organization and Event Listings

Each broad food category has a chapter in this book. Festivals are grouped under the appropriate category based on the primary food highlighted. Within each chapter, the events are listed by date held and then alphabetically. Though we took great effort to be thorough, there may be some events we inadvertently missed.

Each listing includes pertinent details for each festival, including the general date, location, contact information, description of activities, and featured food. In cases where a festival did not have a dedicated website, e-mail, or phone number, we listed the contact information for the local city, Chamber of Commerce, or tourist information bureau. These organizations often provide information for events in their local areas.

Admission prices often change from one year to another. While we have included specific costs when available, please allow for some variation. Public admission fees are coded as follows: Free, $ = $1-$14, $$ = $15-$34, $$$ = $35+.

For those with kids, look for "~ *Great for Kids*" printed beside the festival name. This indicates specific activities (e.g., games, parades, etc.) catering to children.

Various specifics for each festival may not have been available at the time of printing. Every effort was made to contact the festival organizer to verify the information, but we did not receive responses from them all. We opted to include the event regardless, knowing any responsible festival-goer will confirm the event before making plans!

The dates in the listing are general. For example, the date may be listed as "First weekend in March." Consult the companion website (see next section) for the festival calendar for the current year.

Help us keep the festival information accurate. If you find that a festival has been dropped, moved, or changed dates, please let us know so we can update our information. Any new or changed festival information will be posted on the companion website and considered for inclusion in the next edition of the book. Send us an e-mail either via our website contact form or to info@FoodFestGuide.com.

The book also provides directories of the festivals by region, month, and event name (alphabetical). Eat your way through the calendar and across (or up and down) Florida!

How to Use the Companion Website

The companion website (http://www.FoodFestGuide.com) to *Food Fest! Your Complete Guide to Florida's Food Festivals* offers many interesting features that complement the book. Among other things, the website includes a discussion forum, details for upcoming festivals, and a list of the Florida Chambers of Commerce.

Additional bonus features are available if you register on the website and then log in with your user name and password. Registration is free. This special area includes a yearly calendar of festivals so you can plan ahead. The calendar indicates the specific festival dates (e.g., March 10-11, 2006) when available for the current year. Optimally, this information can be printed and placed inside the book for quick reference. Also available to registered users is a listing of new festivals discovered since the printing of the book.

For more information, or to register and activate your account, go to http://www.FoodFestGuide.com. If you would like to send us information or provide feedback, please use the contact form on the website, send us an e-mail at info@FoodFestGuide.com, or drop us a note via the postal service P.O. Box 8598, Seminole, FL 33775. We'd love to hear from you!

2 Seafood Fiesta

If you love seafood, but feel queasy on the waterways, Florida's seafood festivals are your Dramamine. In a state almost completely surrounded by oceans, seafood-related festivals outnumber just about every other category. Florida continually ranks among the top states in fresh seafood production, contributing a significant economic impact to the state. Try Florida's most popular fish—grouper. Floridians catch more than 90 percent of the nation's supply. Or if shellfish better suits your taste, shrimp, the top seafood harvested in Florida by dollar amount and weight, is plentiful. Boil it, grill it, blacken it, eat it raw—whatever your particular fancy, there's a mouthwatering seafood entrée for you!

A woman enjoys her shrimp dinner.

GOODLAND MULLET FESTIVAL

City/County/Region: Marco Island / Collier / Southwest
Location: Stan's Idle Hour Seafood Restaurant in the Goodland community on Marco Island, off State Road 92 at the southeast corner of the island
General Date: 3rd weekend in January
Duration: 3 days
Year Started: 1986
Approx. Attendance: 3,000
Public Admission Fee: Free
Other Fees/Costs: Unavailable
Contact Information: (239) 394-3041, http://www.stansidlehour.net, Alternative contact: (877) 387-2582
Description: Fried and smoked mullet are featured. Events include the coronation of the Buzzard Lope Queen and also a Buzzard Lope Princess day when girls from ages 6 to 16 compete for the title, a trophy, and cash prizes. The Buzzard Lope is a dance based on "The Buzzard Lope Song" composed and sung by the owner of Stan's Idle Hour Restaurant.

BUCKHEAD RIDGE CATFISH FESTIVAL

City/County/Region: Buckhead Ridge / Glades / Southwest
Location: Buckhead Ridge Fire Dept., 678 Hwy 78 W
General Date: Last Saturday in January
Duration: 1 day
Year Started: 1984
Approx. Attendance: Varies
Public Admission Fee: Unknown
Other Fees/Costs: Unavailable

Contact Information: (863) 946-0440, gccommerce@gladesonline.com, http://www.gladesonline.com

Description: Enjoy catfish dinners, craft show, music and entertainment. Sponsored by and fundraiser for the Buckhead Ridge Volunteer Fire Department.

FLORIDA KEYS SEAFOOD FESTIVAL

City/County/Region: Key West / Monroe / Southwest
Location: Bayview Park
General Date: The Saturday before MLK Day in January
Duration: 1 day
Year Started: 2006
Approx. Attendance: Varies
Public Admission Fee: Free
Other Fees/Costs: Unavailable
Contact Information: (305) 292-4501, lindley-cristina@monroecounty-fl.gov, http://www.monroecounty-fl.gov/Pages/MonroeCoFL_News/007CC6A9-000F8513, Alternative contact: Florida Keys Commercial Fishermen's Association, (305) 619-0039, mccf1@comcast.net

Description: Features fresh, local seafood from Florida Keys commercial fishermen. Menu includes lobster, fish, stone crab claws, conch chowder, conch fritters, and conch salad. Entertainment, vendors, and non-profit organizations. Sponsored by the Monroe County Commercial Fishermen Association and the University of Florida's Monroe County Extension Service.

Food Fest! Your Complete Guide to Florida's Food Festivals

EVERGLADES SEAFOOD FESTIVAL ~ *Great for Kids!*

City/County/Region:	Everglades / Collier / Southwest
Location:	Everglades City
General Date:	1st weekend in February
Duration:	3 days
Year Started:	1974
Approx. Attendance:	52,000
Public Admission Fee:	Free
Other Fees/Costs:	Unavailable
Contact Information:	(239) 695-4100, info@evergladesseafoodfestival.com, http://www.evergladesseafoodfestival.com, Alternative contact: (239) 695-3781
Description:	Emphasis on seafood, but lots of other great food including gator nuggets, fish chowder, stone crabs, frog legs, catfish fingers, and indian fry bread. State of the art rides and attractions. Over 150 arts and crafts booths. Live music Saturday and Sunday. No pets or coolers.

JUMBALAYA JAM ~ *Great for Kids!*

City/County/Region:	Melbourne / Brevard / Central East
Location:	Main Pavilion Wickham Park, 2500 Parkway Drive
General Date:	3rd weekend in February
Duration:	3 days
Year Started:	1993
Approx. Attendance:	20,000
Public Admission Fee:	$
Other Fees/Costs:	Admission fee $5, children younger than 6 admitted free with paying adult.

Contact Information: (321) 633-4028, info@brevardparks.com, http://www.fairmanagement.com

Description: Cajun food festival featuring three days of Cajun and blues music, plus rides and lots of Cajun food.

Cortez Commercial Fishing Festival ~ *Great for Kids!*

City/County/Region: Cortez / Manatee / Central West
Location: Cortez Village, 124th St. Ct. West
General Date: 3rd weekend in February
Duration: 2 days
Year Started: 1981
Approx. Attendance: 20,000
Public Admission Fee: $
Other Fees/Costs: Admission to the festival is $2 and children under 12 are free. Buses shuttle visitors from Coquina Beach on the island and at Sugg Middle School to Cortez for $1 each way.
Contact Information: (941) 794-1249, info@cortezfishingfestival.org, http://cortezfishingfestival.org
Description: More seafood than imaginable and, of course, plenty of beer to wash it down with! Live music, nautical arts and crafts, children's activities, and environmental exhibits.

Grant Seafood Festival

City/County/Region: Grant / Brevard / Central East
Location: Grant Community Center
General Date: Last weekend in February
Duration: 2 days

Year Started:	1966
Approx. Attendance:	50,000
Public Admission Fee:	Free
Other Fees/Costs:	Admission and parking are free.
Contact Information:	grantseafoodfestival@yahoo.com, http://www.grantseafoodfestival.com
Description:	Southeast Florida's largest and longest running seafood festival. Over 100 crafters exhibiting, live continuous entertainment, along with a scrumptious menu of succulent seafood (clams, shrimp, scallops, conch, crab, oysters, and more).

HARBOR SOUNDS SEAFOOD & MUSIC FESTIVAL ~ *Great for Kids!*

City/County/Region:	Safety Harbor / Pinellas / Central West
Location:	Safety Harbor Marina Park, 131 S Bayshore Blvd.
General Date:	1st weekend in March
Duration:	2 days
Year Started:	1993
Approx. Attendance:	12,000
Public Admission Fee:	$
Other Fees/Costs:	Admission is $3, free for children 12 and younger.
Contact Information:	(727) 726-2890, info@safetyharborchamber.com, http://www.safetyharborchamber.com
Description:	Live music (rock, blues, oldies), seafood (blackened, grilled, baked and fried), other dishes such as barbecue, jambalaya, gyros, turkey legs, frog legs, alligator and desserts. Arts and crafts, children's activity area, and

family activities. Fundraiser for the Chamber of Commerce and the City of Safety Harbor for scholarship funds, the chamber's operating budget, and educational programs.

CAJUN ZYDECO CRAWFISH FESTIVAL ~ *Great for Kids!*

City/County/Region: St. Petersburg / Pinellas / Central West
Location: Vinoy Park, Fifth Avenue NE and Bayshore Drive
General Date: 2nd weekend in March
Duration: 3 days
Year Started: 2001
Approx. Attendance: 17,000
Public Admission Fee: $
Other Fees/Costs: Tickets are $12 Friday and Sunday, $15 Saturday and $30 for a weekend pass. Tickets available at the gate or Ticketmaster. Food prices range from $2 for a hotdog to $16 for a big Cajun seafood meal.
Contact Information: (813) 986-7978, olcajun@verizon.net, http://www.cajunconnection.org, Alternative contact: (813) 417-7298
Description: Experience Cajun, Creole and Louisiana culture and food with thousands of pounds of crawfish and Louisiana foods including jambalaya, gumbo, crawfish, gator burgers, red beans and rice, pralines and more. Swamp Pop music, food vendors, dancing, arts and crafts, and children's crafts. No pets, coolers or umbrellas allowed inside the festival grounds. Alcoholic beverages will not be allowed outside the festival grounds.

Fort Myers Beach Shrimp Festival ~ *Great for Kids!*

City/County/Region: Fort Myers Beach / Lee / Southwest
Location: Lynn Hall Park on Estero Island
General Date: 2nd weekend in March
Duration: 2 days
Year Started: Unavailable
Approx. Attendance: Varies
Public Admission Fee: Free
Other Fees/Costs: Unavailable
Contact Information: (800) 366-3622, Fortmyers@fortmyers.org, http://www.fortmyers.org/calendar.htm, Alternative contact: Greater Fort Myers Beach Area Chamber of Commerce, http://www.fmbchamber.com, info@fmbchamber.com, (239) 454-7500
Description: A delight for shrimp lovers. Events include a 5-K run on the beach, parade, shrimp boils, and Queen's dance. Sponsored by the Fort Myers Beach Lions Club.

Speckled Perch Festival ~ *Great for Kids!*

City/County/Region: Okeechobee / Okeechobee / Central East
Location: Flagler Park in Downtown Okeechobee, Hwy. 441 and 70
General Date: 2nd weekend in March
Duration: 2 days
Year Started: 1968
Approx. Attendance: 10,000
Public Admission Fee: Free
Other Fees/Costs: Tickets for rodeo (reserved seats) are $14.

Contact Information: (863) 763-6464, chamber@okeechobeechamberofcommerce.com, http://www.okeechobeechamberofcommerce.com

Description: Lots of great food including dinners of fried fish, salad and hush puppies. Seminole Indian food specialties, kettle corn, and more. Festivities include parade, arts and crafts, live entertainment, kids' rides and games, and a vintage car show. About a mile north of Flagler Park is the Cattleman's Rodeo Arena, where a rodeo starts at 2:30 p.m. each day.

PALM BEACH SEAFOOD FESTIVAL ~ *Great for Kids!*

City/County/Region: Palm Beach / Palm Beach / Southeast
Location: Howard Park on the corner of Okeechobee Blvd and Parker
General Date: 3rd weekend in March
Duration: 3 days
Year Started: 1987
Approx. Attendance: 15,000
Public Admission Fee: Free
Other Fees/Costs: Unavailable
Contact Information: (561) 832-6397, rlavenia@fantasma.com, http://www.fantasma.com/special
Description: Features seafood vendors and restaurants from throughout the Southeastern U.S. Live reggae, classic rock and jazz music, arts and crafts exhibits, and a children's area and midway. A portion of the proceeds will benefit local charities.

GREAT ATLANTIC SEAFOOD FESTIVAL ~ *Great for Kids!*

City/County/Region:	Jacksonville / Duval / Northeast
Location:	Sea Walk Pavilion
General Date:	3rd Saturday in March
Duration:	1 day
Year Started:	Unavailable
Approx. Attendance:	Varies
Public Admission Fee:	Unknown
Other Fees/Costs:	Unavailable
Contact Information:	(904) 249-3972, jaxbchweb@jaxbchfl.net, http://www.jaxbeachfestivals.com, Alternative contact: http://www.jaxbch.govoffice.com
Description:	Florida's finest seafood—fried, broiled, boiled, grilled or blackened. Music for everyone, arts and crafts, rides and games for the whole family. Fashion show and 5K run.

MARATHON SEAFOOD FESTIVAL

City/County/Region:	Marathon / Monroe / Southwest
Location:	Marathon Airport, 9400 Overseas Highway
General Date:	3rd or 4th weekend in March
Duration:	2 days
Year Started:	1971
Approx. Attendance:	Varies
Public Admission Fee:	$
Other Fees/Costs:	Children under 12 are admitted free with paying adult. All others pay $5 for admission and a free raffle ticket for a chance to win a chest of seafood valued at $200.
Contact Information:	(305) 743-5417, info@floridakeysmarathon.com, http://www.floridakeysmarathon.com, Chamber of Commerce (800) 842-9580.

Description: Lots of seafood including dolphin, shrimp, lobster, crab, oysters, clams. Also features music, a nautical flea market, marine equipment, boat show, arts and crafts, and airplanes. Sponsored by the Fisherman of Florida—Marathon Chapter and the Greater Marathon Chamber of Commerce.

PLACIDA ROTARY SEAFOOD FESTIVAL ~ *Great for Kids!*

City/County/Region: Placida / Charlotte / Southwest

Location: The Fishery Restaurant, 1300 Fishery Road, on the waters edge where 771 meets 776, just past the traffic light to the Boca Grande Causeway Toll plaza.

General Date: 3rd weekend in March

Duration: 2 days

Year Started: 1998

Approx. Attendance: 12,000

Public Admission Fee: $

Other Fees/Costs: $2 per adult, free for all children under 12. Parking $2 per car across the street from the Fishery Restaurant.

Contact Information: (941) 697-2451, TheFishery@gls3c.com, http://www.seafoodfestival.info, Alternative contact: (941) 697-2313, http://www.placidarotary.com

Description: Offers a variety of tasty seafood such as: Fishery Restaurant traditional gumbo, fried fish and shrimp, Cajun shrimp, Cajun sausage, smoked mullet, blackened grouper, and even some squid, octopus, alligator. Kids activities include crab races, clowns, face painting. Arts and crafts, live music, fishing and pleasure boats on display. Held by the Rotary Club of Placida in partnership with the Fishery Restaurant.

St. Augustine Lions Seafood Festival ~ *Great for Kids!*

City/County/Region: St. Augustine / St. Johns / Northeast
Location: The Events Field at US1 and Castillo Drive directly behind the Visitors Center.
General Date: Mid or end of March
Duration: 3 days
Year Started: 1982
Approx. Attendance: Varies
Public Admission Fee: $
Other Fees/Costs: Donation of $1 is requested.
Contact Information: (904) 829-1753, bigdom61@hotmail.com, http://staugustinelionsclubfl.lionwap.org
Description: Seafood cooked almost any way you can imagine, dessert booths, clowns, magicians, more than 100 arts and crafts booths, the ReMax hot air balloon for rides (weather permitting). Featuring live bluegrass music all weekend, provided by assistance from the Northeast Florida Bluegrass Association. All proceeds for the balloon rides go to the Children's Miracle Network. All proceeds from the festival go to Lions Charities.

Cajun Blues Crawfish Festival

City/County/Region: Palm Beach / Palm Beach / Southeast
Location: Meyer Amphitheater and Flagler Drive, Downtown West Palm Beach
General Date: 1st weekend in April
Duration: 2 days
Year Started: 2005
Approx. Attendance: Varies

Public Admission Fee: Unknown
Other Fees/Costs: Unavailable
Contact Information: (561) 799-7966, info@palmbeachfestivals.com, http://www.palmbeachfestivals.com/cajun/cajunbluescrawfish.php, Alternative contact: (561) 822-1515, http://www.cityofwpb.com/events/events.php
Description: Cajun and Creole Cuisine from regional restaurants, featuring Louisiana style boiled live crawfish to gumbo and beignets. Live music entertainment.

St. Johns River Catfish Festival - *Great for Kids!*

City/County/Region: Crescent City / Putnam / Northeast
Location: Off Highway 17 in Crescent City
General Date: 1st weekend in April
Duration: 2 days
Year Started: 1979
Approx. Attendance: 20,000
Public Admission Fee: Free
Other Fees/Costs: Unavailable
Contact Information: (386) 698-1644, info@catfishfestival.com, http://www.catfishfestival.com, Alternative contact: Crescent City Rotary Club, http://www.crescentcityrotary.org/, info@crescentcityrotary.org
Description: Fried catfish dinners, swamp cabbage, alligator tail, and much more! Arts and crafts, local music acts, 5K run, parade, car show. Sponsored by the Rotary Club of Crescent City.

Spring Fish Fry

City/County/Region: Leesburg / Lake / Central
Location: Grounds of the Historic Mote-Morris House
General Date: 1st Thursday in April
Duration: 1 day
Year Started: 1997
Approx. Attendance: Varies
Public Admission Fee: Unknown
Other Fees/Costs: Ticketed event.
Contact Information: (352) 365-0053, info@leesburgpartnership.com, http://www.leesburgpartnership.com
Description: Featuring southern cooking at its finest! Fresh fried fish, steamed oysters, corn on the cob, collard greens, corn bread, navy beans, key lime pie, hush puppies and beverages including iced tea, soft drinks, beer, wine and bar. Sponsored by the Leesburg Partnership.

Cajun Cafe on the Bayou Crawfish Festival

City/County/Region: Pinellas Park / Pinellas / Central West
Location: Cajun Cafe on the Bayou restaurant, 8101 Park Blvd.
General Date: 2nd weekend in April
Duration: 3 days
Year Started: 1998
Approx. Attendance: Varies
Public Admission Fee: $
Other Fees/Costs: Admission is $10 per day, 3-day pass $20 (purchase at gate), Children under 12 free. Free parking.
Contact Information: (727) 546-6732, paulunwin59@hotmail.com, http://cajuncafeonthebayou.olm.net

Description: Lots of good Cajun food including Cajun Café's fresh boiled crawfish, gumbo, jambalaya, and more. Live music featuring Cajun bands. Free Cajun and Zydeco dance lessons!

NATIONAL SHRIMP AND OYSTER FESTIVAL ~ *Great for Kids!*

City/County/Region: Panama City / Bay / Northwest
Location: Historic St. Andrews area at Carl Grey Park
General Date: 2nd weekend in April
Duration: 3 days
Year Started: Unavailable
Approx. Attendance: Varies
Public Admission Fee: $
Other Fees/Costs: Admission is $3, free for ages 6 and under.
Contact Information: (850) 784-9542, gelynch@bellsouth.net, http://www.emeraldcoastevents.com/festivals.htm
Description: A traditional seafood festival along the bay. Travel by car or boat. Children's entertainment and activities, arts and crafts from across the nation, entertainment around the clock. Culminating with a grand fireworks exhibition on Saturday night.

RAJUNCAJUN CRAWFISH FESTIVAL

City/County/Region: Orlando / Orange / Central
Location: Isle of Pine's South Beach, 13040 Lake Mary Jane Rd.
General Date: 4th Saturday in April
Duration: 1 day
Year Started: 1990
Approx. Attendance: 500

Food Fest! Your Complete Guide to Florida's Food Festivals

Public Admission Fee: $$$
Other Fees/Costs: Presale tickets only. $35 for general admission, $15 for ages 8-12, Free for ages 7 and under. This event always sells out in advance and they do not sell tickets at the gate. Price includes entertainment, food and non-alcholic beverages.
Contact Information: (407) 737-9049, sales@crawfishcoofcentralflainc.com, http://www.crawfishcoofcentralflainc.com
Description: Price includes all you can eat authentic Louisiana cuisine (e.g., Crawfish Boiled New Orleans Style, Royal Red Shrimp Head-on Louisiana Style, Black Bayou Double-Dipped Fried Chicken), all you can drink (non-alcoholic beverages), live cajun music, arts and crafts. BYOB alcoholic drinks.

SHRIMP FEST ~ *Great for Kids!*

City/County/Region: Ponce Inlet / Volusia / Central East
Location: Inlet Harbor Restaurant & Marina, 133 Inlet Harbor Road
General Date: 4th weekend in April
Duration: 2 days
Year Started: 1998
Approx. Attendance: 5,000
Public Admission Fee: Free
Other Fees/Costs: Unavailable
Contact Information: (386) 767-8755, info@inletharbor.com, http://www.inletharbor.com/events.html
Description: Hosted by Inlet Harbor and benefits the Daytona Beach Culinary Institute. Students

prepare shrimp dishes that are judged by local dignitaries. Continuous live music and children's activities throughout both days. Live music from local bands includes music for all ages. Kid's activities include face painting, balloons, clowns, hermit crab races, limbo, and a shrimp toss. Part of the proceeds will be given in the form of scholarships to the culinary students.

Pompano Beach Seafood Festival ~ *Great for Kids!*

City/County/Region: Pompano Beach / Broward / Southeast
Location: East end of Atlantic Boulevard where the street ends and the beach sand begins
General Date: Last full weekend in April
Duration: 3 days
Year Started: 1985
Approx. Attendance: 35,000
Public Admission Fee: $
Other Fees/Costs: Admission $10, kids under 10 free.
Contact Information: (954) 570-7785, goodshows@bellsouth.net, http://www.pompanobeachseafoodfestival.com, Alternative contact: (954) 941-2940, http://www.pompanobeachchamber.com, pompano@pompanobeachchamber.com
Description: Food court including raw bar, fresh fish, shellfish, seafood pasta, cajun dishes, fritters, and more. Concerts on ocean side stage featuring national and local acts, kid's area fun zone, arts and crafts.

Isle Of Eight Flags Shrimp Festival - *Great for Kids!*

City/County/Region:	Fernandina Beach / Nassau / Northeast
Location:	Historic downtown Centre St. business district
General Date:	1st weekend in May
Duration:	3 days
Year Started:	1963
Approx. Attendance:	120,000
Public Admission Fee:	Free
Other Fees/Costs:	$5 to park per vehicle.
Contact Information:	(904) 261-3248, 4info@shrimpfestival.com, http://www.shrimpfestival.com
Description:	All kinds of shrimp dishes prepared onsite by over 30 local organizations, juried fine arts and crafts, antiques, parade, pirate invasion, fireworks, live music entertainment on various stages, kid's fun zone, Miss Shrimp Festival scholarship pageant. A Southeast Tourism Society Top 20 Event.

Pensacola Crawfish Creole Fiesta - *Great for Kids!*

City/County/Region:	Pensacola / Escambia / Northwest
Location:	Bartram Park, downtown
General Date:	1st weekend in May
Duration:	3 days
Year Started:	1983
Approx. Attendance:	9,000
Public Admission Fee:	$
Other Fees/Costs:	Admission is $5 for adults, free for children under 12.

Contact Information: (850) 433-6512, info@FiestaofFiveFlags.org, http://www.fiestaoffiveflags.org/crawfish.htm

Description: One of the largest crawfish boils in state. In addition to crawfish, other traditional Cajun fare is available such as spicy chicken, red beans and rice, jambalaya and etouffee. Bayou Country and Louisiana musicians entertain. Many activities in the children's area.

PANACEA BLUE CRAB FESTIVAL ~ *Great for Kids!*

City/County/Region: Panacea / Wakulla / North Central

Location: Wooley Park which stretches along Dickerson Bay just off Coastal Highway 98 in the heart of Panacea

General Date: 1st Saturday in May

Duration: 1 day

Year Started: 1976

Approx. Attendance: 20,000

Public Admission Fee: $

Other Fees/Costs: Admission is $3 per person and parking is free.

Contact Information: (850) 984-2722, info@bluecrabfest.com, http://www.bluecrab-festival.com

Description: Variety of food vendors, parade, arts and crafts, live music and exhibits. Demonstrations and contests including crab picking, crab trap pulling, and a mullet toss. A fireworks display concludes the festivities. A food court with tables and seating is available, but attendees may also bring folding chairs to enjoy the music and fireworks.

COTEE RIVER SEAFOOD FESTIVAL AND BOAT SHOW ~ *Great for Kids!*

City/County/Region: New Port Richey / Pasco / Central West
Location: Sims Park and Orange Lake areas, downtown
General Date: Mothers Day weekend in May
Duration: 2 days
Year Started: 2000
Approx. Attendance: 10,000
Public Admission Fee: $
Other Fees/Costs: Nominal admission of $5 is charged for Saturday evening. A $2 donation per person to enter the festival is requested to help Greater New Port Richey Main Street bring events to downtown.
Contact Information: (727) 842-8066, info@nprmainstreet.com, http://www.newportricheymainstreet.com
Description: Seafood, crafts, boats and Xtreme Family Fun Zone for kids. Music by local, regional, and national bands. Activities and games for kids, boat tours up the Cotee River in Downtown New Port Richey, a wide variety of food (primarily seafood) and beverage vendors, as well as an arts and crafts fair featuring a myriad of art forms, primarily focusing on nautical and natural themed hand-crafted products. Nominal admission charged for Saturday evening. A small donation per person to enter the festival is requested to help Greater New Port Richey Main Street bring events to downtown.

DAYTONA BEACH BAYOU BOIL ~ *Great for Kids!*

City/County/Region: Daytona Beach / Volusia / Central East
Location: Main Street

General Date: 3rd or 4th Saturday in May
Duration: 1 day
Year Started: 1999
Approx. Attendance: 15,000
Public Admission Fee: Unknown
Other Fees/Costs: Unavailable
Contact Information: (386) 255-9300, FJDeMarchi@hotmail.com, http://www.wkro.fm, Phone number listed is 93.1 Kro Country - dial extension #383. Alternative contact: http://www.daytonabeachcvb.org, tboyd@daytonabeachcvb.org, or Daytona Beach area's official visitor information Web site at http://www.daytonabeach.com
Description: Annual kick-off to summer with the big easy coming to Main Street. Also kicks off hurricane season with a district-wide bartender contest for the hurricane drink with a Daytona twist. Drinks on sale at the event. Up to 14 bands with a Cajun slant. Multiple food courts with crawfish stands at each. Kid's games, hot rod show, merchant sidewalk sales, and more.

PALATKA BLUE CRAB FESTIVAL ~ *Great for Kids!*

City/County/Region: Palatka / Putnam / Northeast
Location: Downtown Palatka
General Date: Memorial Day weekend
Duration: 4 days
Year Started: 1989
Approx. Attendance: 200,000
Public Admission Fee: Free
Other Fees/Costs: Unavailable

Contact Information: (386) 325-4406, info@bluecrabfestival.com, http://www.bluecrabfestival.com

Description: Florida Seafood Cookoff State Championship (chowder and gumbo categories), live music performances, fine arts show, antiques show and sale, arts and crafts, Memorial Day parade and ceremony, kids' rides, many other activities and games. Fireworks Friday night kicks off the festival.

CLAMERICA CELEBRATION ~ *Great for Kids!*

City/County/Region: Cedar Key / Levy / North Central
Location: City Park, 2nd Street
General Date: July 4th
Duration: 1 day
Year Started: 2004
Approx. Attendance: Varies
Public Admission Fee: Free
Other Fees/Costs: Unavailable
Contact Information: (352) 543-5057, LNST@ifas.ufl.edu, http://shellfish.ifas.ufl.edu
Description: Clams any way you like them—steamed, on the half shell, in chowder or fritters. Other landlubber's food, too. Clamania events include a clam hunt, clam shucking demos, clam cook-off, clam bag races, clam boat tours, and many more with prizes galore! Also features live music and fireworks. Hosted by the Cedar Key Aquaculture Association.

Gulf County Scallop Festival

City/County/Region:	Port Saint Joe / Gulf / Northwest
Location:	Port St. Joe
General Date:	Last weekend in August
Duration:	2 days
Year Started:	1997
Approx. Attendance:	Varies
Public Admission Fee:	Free
Other Fees/Costs:	Unavailable
Contact Information:	(850) 227-1223, sandra@gulfchamber.org, http://www.gulfchamber.org
Description:	Local scallops, music, entertainment, arts and crafts. Sponsored by the Port St. Joe Chamber of Commerce.

Aug 7,8, 2010

Seafood & Mini Wine Fest ~ *Great for Kids!*

City/County/Region:	Sandestin / Okaloosa / Northwest
Location:	The Market Shops at Sandestin
General Date:	1st weekend in September
Duration:	2 days
Year Started:	Unavailable
Approx. Attendance:	Varies
Public Admission Fee:	$
Other Fees/Costs:	Tickets to wine tasting are $12 in advance and $15 at the door. Admission is free to the concerts and the children's activities.
Contact Information:	(850) 267-8092, specialevents@sandestin.com, http://www.sandestin.com/sandestin_sub_1.asp?sub1_id=135
Description:	Wine lovers can sample fifty different wines during the Mini Wine Tasting. Also a bounty of fresh seafood, live music, and children's events.

Food Fest! Your Complete Guide to Florida's Food Festivals

SEBASTIAN CLAMBAKE LAGOON FESTIVAL

City/County/Region: Sebastian / Indian River / Central East
Location: Riverview Park at the corner of US Hwy 1 and CR 512
General Date: In the fall (September, October, or November)
Duration: 3 days
Year Started: Unavailable
Approx. Attendance: Varies
Public Admission Fee: Free
Other Fees/Costs: Unavailable
Contact Information: (772) 589-5490, city@cityofsebastian.org, http://www.cityofsebastian.org, Alternative contact: (888) 881-7568
Description: Clams prepared any way you can imagine. Wacky raft races on the Indian River, boat show, chowder cook-off, kayak poker run, clammer-slammer beach volleyball tournament and the Colgate Country Showdown.

[handwritten: Nov 5-7, 2010   www.sebastianclambake.org]

HOLLYWOOD BEACH CLAMBAKE ~ *Great for Kids!*

City/County/Region: Hollywood / Broward / Southeast
Location: Hollywood Beach Broadwalk, north and south of Johnson Street Bandshell (between Hollywood Boulevard and Garfield Street)
General Date: Most recently 3rd weekend in September. In the past, it's also been held in July and August.
Duration: 3 days
Year Started: 2002
Approx. Attendance: 35,000
Public Admission Fee: Free
Other Fees/Costs: Free or paid parking available.

2 - Seafood Fiesta

Contact Information: (954) 924-2980, Events@ProjectMarketing.com, http://www.hollywoodbeachclambake.com

Description: Clambake Pavilion, children's activities in the Beach Kids Play Zone, live music on three stages, Taste of Florida Seafood on the Broadwalk, Best Chowder Contest, children's costume contests, Full Moon Beach Bonfire and Volunteer Beach Cleanup. Ocean-theme vendors and arts and crafts line the Broadwalk. Presented by the City of Hollywood and its Hollywood Beach Community Redevelopment Agency (http://www.hollywoodbeachcra.org/), and produced by Fiesta Tropicale of Hollywood, Inc. The dates for this festival has changed often. It's usually held in the summer or early fall (e.g., July, August, September). Make sure you contact them for the current year's schedule.

FALL SEAFOOD AND PIRATE FEST ~ *Great for Kids!*

City/County/Region: Panama City / Bay / Northwest
Location: Historic St. Andrews area on the St. Andrews Marina and the surrounding area.
General Date: 4th weekend in September
Duration: 3 days
Year Started: Unavailable
Approx. Attendance: Varies
Public Admission Fee: Unknown
Other Fees/Costs: Unavailable
Contact Information: gelynch@bellsouth.net, http://www.emeraldcoastevents.com/festivals.htm
Description: Seafood festival with a pirate twist held along the bay. Travel by car or boat. Children's

31

entertainment and activities. Arts and crafts from across the nation. Entertainment around the clock.

PENSACOLA SEAFOOD FESTIVAL

City/County/Region: Pensacola / Escambia / Northwest
Location: Seville Square, Fountain Park, Bartram Park
General Date: Last weekend in September
Duration: 3 days
Year Started: 1977
Approx. Attendance: Varies
Public Admission Fee: Free
Other Fees/Costs: Unavailable
Contact Information: (850) 433-6512, info@FiestaofFiveFlags.org, http://www.fiestaoffiveflags.org/seafood.htm
Description: Delicious seafood, both traditional and gourmet recipes, such as fried mullet, crabmeat puffs with Monterey sauce, crawfish etouffe, and seafood pita.

FLORIDA CRACKER OYSTER FESTIVAL

City/County/Region: Orlando / Orange / Central
Location: Isle Of Pines South Beach, 13040 Lake Mary Jane Rd.
General Date: 4th Saturday in September
Duration: 1 day
Year Started: 2004
Approx. Attendance: 200
Public Admission Fee: $$

Other Fees/Costs: Presale tickets only. Tickets are $25 for adults, $10 for kids 8-12, Free for kids 7 and under. Admission includes "All-U-Can-Eat-N-Drink" (included beverages are non-alcoholic only).

Contact Information: (407) 384-9211, sales@ crawfishcoofcentralflainc.com, http://www.crawfishcoofcentralflainc.com/Florida_Cracker_Oyster_Festival.html

Description: Assortment of Louisiana and Florida foods including oysters on the half shell, Bourbon Street fried oysters, French Quarter fried catfish, Black Bayou buffalo wings, and much more. Event hosted by the Isle of Pines Property Owners Association, Inc.

DESTIN SEAFOOD FESTIVAL ~ *Great for Kids!*

City/County/Region: Destin / Okaloosa / Northwest

Location: Morgan Sports Center, located behind City Hall at 1121 Airport Road

General Date: 1st full weekend in October

Duration: 3 days

Year Started: 1979

Approx. Attendance: 21,000

Public Admission Fee: $

Other Fees/Costs: Charge of $5 per person for admission the festival for the entire weekend. Children under 12 are admitted free. Can purchase buttons in advance via PDF order form on website, or call the Destin Area Chamber (see Contact Info). Site parking is limited, so the Destin Seafood Festival offers free parking and free shuttle service to and from various Destin-area locations.

Contact Information: (850) 837-6241, mail@destinchamber.com, http://www.destinseafoodfestival.org, Alternative contact: http://www.destinchamber.com

Description: Food court with great food, more than 100 arts and crafts vendors, kids activities, and concerts.

HERNANDO BEACH SEAFOOD FESTIVAL

City/County/Region: Hernando Beach / Hernando / Central West
Location: Hernando Beach
General Date: 2nd weekend in October
Duration: 2 days
Year Started: 1983
Approx. Attendance: 5,000
Public Admission Fee: Free
Other Fees/Costs: Admission is free. Parking is $2.
Contact Information: (352) 688-7431, sally@hbyachtclub.com, http://www.hbyachtclub.com, Alternative contact: bhaag@tampabay.rr.com
Description: Seafood samplings from area restaurants, entertainment, arts and crafts, vendors, games, and more.

INDIAN SUMMER SEAFOOD FESTIVAL ~ *Great for Kids!*

City/County/Region: Panama City Beach / Bay / Northwest
Location: Frank Brown Park, 16200 Panama City Beach Parkway
General Date: 2nd weekend in October
Duration: 3 days
Year Started: 1981
Approx. Attendance: Varies

Public Admission Fee: $
Other Fees/Costs: Adults admission $10 for day pass, $5 for children under 12 years old. $25 for adult weekend pass.
Contact Information: (850) 233-5070, info@800pcbeach.com, http://www.thebeachloversbeach.com, Alternative contact: (800)-PCBEACH, http://www.panamacitybeachguide.net/seafood_festival.html
Description: Diverse group of food vendors, live entertainment, arts and crafts, children's activities, exhibits and demonstrations.

BOGGY BAYOU MULLET FESTIVAL ~ *Great for Kids!*

City/County/Region: Niceville / Okaloosa / Northwest
Location: Hwy 85. N. at College Blvd.
General Date: 3rd weekend in October
Duration: 3 days
Year Started: 1976
Approx. Attendance: 100,000
Public Admission Fee: $
Other Fees/Costs: Admission is $6 for age 12-adult, $1 for children under age 12. Admission price includes all entertainment.
Contact Information: (850) 729-4545, lmason@niceville.org, http://www.cityofniceville.org
Description: Festival paying homage to the mullet, a bottom-dwelling fish that inhabits Florida's local bayous. Food includes mullet and fried gator tail. Arts and crafts, live music entertainment, pageant and cross country run. Family fun includes clowns, ponies, snakes and other stuff! Sunday is Family Day (that means no beer).

Cedar Key Seafood Festival

City/County/Region:	Cedar Key / Levy / North Central
Location:	2nd. Street and City Park
General Date:	3rd full weekend in October
Duration:	2 days
Year Started:	Unavailable
Approx. Attendance:	40,000
Public Admission Fee:	Free
Other Fees/Costs:	Unavailable
Contact Information:	(352) 543-5600, info@cedarkey.org, http://www.cedarkey.org
Description:	Large arts and crafts show and a variety of seafood (and other things) prepared and sold by Cedar Key's local non-profit organizations. Live music at various locations around town. Sponsored by the Cedar Key Chamber of Commerce.

Leepa-Rattner Museum of Art Stone Crab Fest ~ *Great for Kids!*

City/County/Region:	Tarpon Springs / Pinellas / Central West
Location:	Tarpon Springs Yacht Club
General Date:	2nd weekend of stone crab season (which opens October 15th)
Duration:	1 day
Year Started:	2003
Approx. Attendance:	150
Public Admission Fee:	$$$
Other Fees/Costs:	Admission is $75 per person, children under 12 get in free with an adult.
Contact Information:	(727) 712-5222, LRMAPR@spcollege.edu, http://www.spcollege.edu/museum

Description: Celebrate the opening of stone crab season with crab fest. (Stone crab season in Florida runs from October 15th to May 15.) Lots of food, music, kids' activities. Proceeds benefit Leepa-Rattner Museum of Art.

Stone Crab Fest

City/County/Region: Summerland Key / Monroe / Southwest
Location: Parking lot of Fish Cutters Restaurant at Mile marker 25 of the Overseas Highway, that's just 25 miles north of Key West, on US 1, Mile Marker 25
General Date: 1st Sunday after October 15th
Duration: 1 day
Year Started: 2004
Approx. Attendance: Varies
Public Admission Fee: Unknown
Other Fees/Costs: Unavailable
Contact Information: (305) 745-9974
Description: Plenty of Florida stone crab. Event features live entertainment.

Stone Crab, Seafood, and Wine Festival

City/County/Region: Longboat Key / Manatee / Central West
Location: The Colony Beach and Tennis Resort
General Date: Last weekend in October
Duration: 4 days
Year Started: 1990
Approx. Attendance: 125
Public Admission Fee: $$$
Other Fees/Costs: Tickets are $70 and up, depending on event.

Contact Information: (941) 383-6464, scswf@colonyfl.com, http://www.colonybeachresort.com/stonecrab

Description: Join the nation's top chefs and vintners for a weekend of culinary demonstrations, gala tastings on the beach, and an exquisite chef's collaboration dinner. Early reservations are recommended. Festival package price includes accommodations, welcome gift, reception and gala dinner and dance.

FRENCHY'S STONE CRAB FESTIVAL

City/County/Region: Clearwater Beach / Pinellas / Central West
Location: Clearwater Beach at Frenchy's Seafood Restaurants
General Date: 4th weekend in October
Duration: 3 days
Year Started: 1985
Approx. Attendance: Varies
Public Admission Fee: Free
Other Fees/Costs: Stone crabs sold by the pound.
Contact Information: (727) 449-2729, info@frenchysonline.com, http://www.frenchysonline.com
Description: Stone crab claw festival marking the beginning of the season. Folks line up at all the Frenchy's restaurants (Original, Rockaway, Salt Water and South Beach) for a claws and beer (tents are erected to handle the overflow). Live music. Go early in the weekend to ensure claw availability!

John's Pass Seafood Festival ~ *Great for Kids!*

City/County/Region: Madeira Beach / Pinellas / Central West
Location: John's Pass Village and Boardwalk, 129th Avenue and Gulf Boulevard
General Date: Last full weekend in October
Duration: 2 days
Year Started: 2002
Approx. Attendance: 10,000
Public Admission Fee: Free
Other Fees/Costs: Unavailable
Contact Information: (727) 397-8764, kmcdole@friendly-fish.com, http://www.johnspass.com/specialevents.cfm
Description: Honoring the grouper capital of the world! Fresh local seafood prepared in a variety of recipes along with shrimp, crab and an assortment of other seafood favorites. Children's play area, live music, and entertainment! Over 100 local artists display their talents in the arts and craft show.

Florida Seafood Festival ~ *Great for Kids!*

City/County/Region: Apalachicola / Franklin / Northwest
Location: Battery Park
General Date: 1st weekend in November
Duration: 2 days
Year Started: 1964
Approx. Attendance: 40,000
Public Admission Fee: $
Other Fees/Costs: Admission is $5, kids under 12 free. Free admission on Friday.
Contact Information: (888) 653-8011, info@FloridaSeafoodFestival.com, http://www.floridaseafoodfestival.com

Description: State's Oldest Maritime Exhibit. Delicious seafood and seafood-related events and displays. Events include oyster eating and oyster shucking contests. Selection of festival queen and king, King Retsyo (oyster spelled backwards) who symbolizes Apalachicola Bay and the bounty harvested by the seafood industry. Other activities include arts and crafts exhibits, parade, 5k Redfish Run, and a Blessing of the Fleet.

RUSKIN SEAFOOD FESTIVAL - *Great for Kids!*

City/County/Region: Ruskin / Hillsborough / Central West
Location: E.G. Simmons Park, 2401 19th Ave. NW
General Date: 1st weekend in November
Duration: 2 days
Year Started: 1989
Approx. Attendance: 14,000
Public Admission Fee: $
Other Fees/Costs: Admission is $5 for adults, $4 for Seniors, children under 12 Free.
Contact Information: (813) 645-3808, ruskinchamber@earthlink.net, http://www.ruskinchamber.org/rccsff
Description: Alcohol free festival that includes seafood, a children's court, a boat show, displays by local businesses, and entertainment. Funds raised support the chamber's economic and community development programs with a portion of the proceeds going to Friends Of The Park.

HUDSON SEAFEST – *Great for Kids!*

City/County/Region:	Hudson / Pasco / Central West
Location:	USA Flea Market at US 19 and SR 52
General Date:	3rd weekend in November
Duration:	3 days
Year Started:	1984
Approx. Attendance:	40,000
Public Admission Fee:	Free
Other Fees/Costs:	Tickets required for Grouper Dinners and for the carnival.
Contact Information:	(727) 233-1137, info@hudsonseafest.com, http://www.hudsonseafest.com, Alternative contact: Hudson Seafest, Inc., (727) 919-3866, iisaacson@hudsonseafest.com
Description:	Big draw to this event is the grouper dinner. More than 2,000 pounds of grouper is ordered for the cookout. Plenty of other seafood also available. Also enjoy musical entertainment, arts and crafts, a carnival, KidZone, sailboat races, and a fishing tournament. Nominal parking donation requested. The Seafest was created by the late Harold Vinecour to raise money for building sidewalks, planting trees, granting scholarships and making donations to a long list of local organizations. Donations also go to many Pasco County charities.

3 Carnivore's Delight

Enter a low-carb diet lover's paradise. Meat, meat, and more meat—we don't need no stinkin' sides! Floridians don't fear the heat—not in our climate and not in our food. We love chili, barbecue, ribs, and—well, you get the picture.

If there's a competitor in you, stack your favorite recipe up against others and enter a barbecue contest or chili cookoff. But don't think you can simply whip up Grandma's secret recipe and enter it. Most chili events are sanctioned by either the International Chili Society (ICS) or the Chili Appreciation Society International (CASI). Both provide rules, membership structure, and competition fees for chili cookoffs. But if you're more interested in eating chili than cooking it, don't despair. After the judging, the contestants typically provide samples to the public for nominal fees.

Two pots are better than one when it comes to chili!

For particular chili or barbecue listings that don't have a dedicated website, check the Florida Chili page (http://www.floridachili.com) or the Florida Barbecue Association page (http://www.flbbq.org). They may have specific information regarding the cookoff (e.g., if it's a sanctioned event, pertinent rules, entry fees, etc.).

If chili or barbecue isn't your thing, there's plenty other food festivals for carnivores. Try the frog leg festival. It's worth it just to say you went! But make sure you really try them—how else will you know if they taste like chicken?

CENTRAL FLORIDA BBQ FESTIVAL ~ *Great for Kids!*

City/County/Region:	Sebring / Highlands / Central
Location:	Sebring
General Date:	1st weekend in January
Duration:	2 days
Year Started:	Unavailable
Approx. Attendance:	Varies
Public Admission Fee:	Free
Other Fees/Costs:	Contest entry fees are $25 or $50 depending on division. No charge for People's Choice division. Teams sell samples in exchange for "pig bucks" (which are exchanged for 70 cents on the dollar).
Contact Information:	(863) 382-2255, info@hcfair.net, http://www.hcfair.net/BBQPage.htm
Description:	Barbecue cook-off featuring twelve hours of BBQ with various categories (chicken, ribs, pork, brisket, and kids) and cash prizes. Also a people's choice where the public can taste and cast their vote for the best BBQ. Other competitions include best booth and hog calling.

GREAT SOUTHERN GUMBO COOK-OFF ~ *Great for Kids!*

City/County/Region: Sandestin / Okaloosa / Northwest
Location: The Market Shops at Sandestin
General Date: 3rd Saturday in January
Duration: 1 day
Year Started: 1990
Approx. Attendance: 2,100
Public Admission Fee: $
Other Fees/Costs: Tickets are $15 per person the day of the event.
Contact Information: (850) 267-8092, specialevents@sandestin.com, http://www.sandestin.com/sandestin_sub_2.asp?sub2_id=369
Description: Taste gumbo from area restaurants then vote for your favorites. Door prizes, kid's events, and live music.

JIM'S CHILI COOKOFF

City/County/Region: St. Petersburg / Pinellas / Central West
Location: Jim's Harley-Davidson, 2805 54th Avenue N.
General Date: In January
Duration: 1 day
Year Started: 2006
Approx. Attendance: Varies
Public Admission Fee: Free
Other Fees/Costs: Contest entry fee $10. $5 for all the chili you can eat.
Contact Information: (727) 527-9672, robinernst@jimshd.com, http://www.jimshd.com/home.html
Description: Chili cook-off (fee to enter). Contact Jim's to sign up and request a copy of the rules. Prizes given for 1st, 2nd, and 3rd place! For non-

competitors, a small fee entitles you to all the chili you can eat. Event also includes vendors and a DJ. Proceeds go to charity.

SUNSHINE REGIONAL CHILI COOK-OFF ~ *Great for Kids!*

City/County/Region:	Kissimmee / Osceola / Central
Location:	Kissimmee Lakefront Park
General Date:	3rd Saturday in January
Duration:	1 day
Year Started:	Unavailable
Approx. Attendance:	10,000
Public Admission Fee:	Unknown
Other Fees/Costs:	Contest entry fee for chili is $30 for International Chili Society (ICS) members, $72 for non-members. $20 for Chili Verde, $15 for Salsa.
Contact Information:	(407) 518-2364, parks@kissimmee.org, http://www.kissimmee.org/w_dept_parks.cfm?id=407, Alternative contact: (407) 518-2501
Description:	International Chili Society (ICS) sanctioned chili cook-off which attracts competitors through out the state of Florida and as far away as Colorado. Winner earns a cash prize and an automatic bid to the I.C.S.'s World Championship Cook-Off in Nevada. This event features free chili samples, live music, kids activities, arts and crafts and food festival.

FELLSMERE FROG LEG FESTIVAL ~ *Great for Kids!*

City/County/Region:	Fellsmere / Indian River / Central East
Location:	City Hall in Fellsmere, 2 Miles West of I 95 on SR # 512 exit # 156 (# 69)

General Date: Begins 3rd Thursday in January
Duration: 4 days
Year Started: Unavailable
Approx. Attendance: Varies
Public Admission Fee: Free
Other Fees/Costs: Free parking. Dinners range from $8-$13.
Contact Information: (772) 571-0116, Froglegfestival@hotmail.com, http://www.froglegfestival.com
Description: Frog leg and gator tail dinners, live entertainment, midway games and rides, contests, arts and crafts.

SUNCOAST CHILI COOKOFF

City/County/Region: Tarpon Springs / Pinellas / Central West
Location: Boys & Girls Club, 111 W. Lime St.
General Date: 3rd Saturday in January
Duration: 1 day
Year Started: 2005
Approx. Attendance: Varies
Public Admission Fee: Unknown
Other Fees/Costs: Contest entry fee is $20 in advance, $25 the day of the cook-off.
Contact Information: (727) 937-0320, djanisz@yahoo.com, Alternative contact: (800) 940-0320
Description: Chili cook-off benefiting Boys & Girls Club. The event is sanctioned by CASI, so those cooking sanctioned chili must follow CASI rules and compete to qualify for the International Chili Cook-off. There's also an "open" category for the everyday cook (no rules). Other activities include car and motorcycle show, craft vendors, food vendors, and live entertainment.

Lakeland Pig Festival ~ *Great for Kids!*

City/County/Region: Lakeland / Polk / Central
Location: Tiger Town and Joker Marchant Stadium, 2301 Lakeland Hills Boulevard
General Date: Last weekend in January
Duration: 1 day
Year Started: 1997
Approx. Attendance: 30,000
Public Admission Fee: Free
Other Fees/Costs: Contest entry fees are $35 for Kids-Q division, $100 for Backyard division, $250 for Professional division. Attendees can purchase BBQ bucks to try food from the various cooks.
Contact Information: (863) 519-3082, gbrown@candcbank.com, http://www.lakelandpigfestival.com
Description: Various adult and children's cooking competitions, BBQ judging classes, cooking demonstrations, children's play areas, entertainment. Benefits charitable organizations in Polk County.

99.9 Kiss Country Regional Chili Cookoff

City/County/Region: Pembroke Pines / Broward / Southeast
Location: C.B. Smith Park, 900 Flamingo Rd.
General Date: Last Sunday in January
Duration: 1 day
Year Started: Unavailable
Approx. Attendance: Varies
Public Admission Fee: $$$
Other Fees/Costs: Tickets are $32 in advance and are available through Ticketmaster, Albertson's

Supermarkets, Grif's Western, The Roundup, CD Heaven West, Sunset Western, OK Feed, Robbie's Feed & Supply and all Dade County Pet Supermarket locations. If available, tickets the day of show are $37. Cookoff entry fee is $125 or $167, depending on category.

Contact Information: (800) 940-7642, info@showmanagement.com, http://www.wkis.com/index.php?page=71, Alternative contact: (954) 764-7642

Description: Chili cook-off benefiting Boys & Girls Clubs of Broward County. Live concerts by national country music acts.

POLICE, FIREFIGHTER, & EMS CHILI COOK OFF

City/County/Region: Winter Haven / Polk / Central
Location: Florida Citrus Festival 210 Cypress Garden Blvd.
General Date: Last Sunday in January
Duration: 1 day
Year Started: 2004
Approx. Attendance: Varies
Public Admission Fee: $
Other Fees/Costs: Must pay gate admission of $7 to the Florida Citrus Festival. Kids age 3 and under free. Contest entry fee $15.
Contact Information: (863) 292-9810, michelle@citrusfestival.com, http://citrusfestival.com/home/index.php?opion=com_content&task=view&id=18&Itemid=27
Description: Chili cook-off during the Florida Citrus Festival. Traditional red and chili verde categories. Judges and a "Peoples Choice" award. All awards go to charity.

GREAT NORTHWEST RIB & FAMILY FEST ~ *Great for Kids!*

City/County/Region: Tampa / Hillsborough / Central West
Location: Sickles High School in Citrus Park
General Date: 1st weekend in February
Duration: 3 days
Year Started: 2006
Approx. Attendance: Varies
Public Admission Fee: Free
Other Fees/Costs: Unavailable
Contact Information: (813) 884-5344, dpaul@utbchamber.com, http://www.oldsmarchamber.org/process.cfm?pageID=57
Description: Rib cook-off where the public can buy ribs from vendors and vote for their favorite one. Events include a talent contest, carnival and midway, arts and crafts show, and musical acts. Co-sponsored by Sickles High School and the Upper Tampa Bay Regional Chamber of Commerce. Proceeds support the Chamber's education foundation which provides college scholarships to graduates of area high schools.

GRILLIN & CHILLIN ON MAIN WAUCHULA ~ *Great for Kids!*

City/County/Region: Wauchula / Hardee / Central
Location: Main St., Wauchula
General Date: 1st weekend in February
Duration: 2 days
Year Started: 2005
Approx. Attendance: Varies
Public Admission Fee: Free
Other Fees/Costs: Contest entry fee required.

Contact Information: (863) 767-0330, info@MainStreetWauchula.com, http://www.mainstreetwauchula.com, Alternative contact: mainstreetwau@earthlink.net

Description: Barbecue cook-off held in conjunction with the Cracker Heritage Festival. Other festival activities include Heritage and Civil War re-enactors, auctions, drawings, Farmer's Market, entertainment, arts and crafts, and the Kid's Korner.

'Do It At The Line' Super Chili Bowl Cookoff

City/County/Region: Pensacola / Escambia / Northwest
Location: Flora-Bama Lounge & Package
General Date: 1st Saturday in February
Duration: 1 day
Year Started: Unavailable
Approx. Attendance: Varies
Public Admission Fee: Unknown
Other Fees/Costs: Contest entry fee of $50 entitles your team (2-person) to one souvenir T-shirt (limit 2) plus free draft beer and other party favors. Tickets for samples will be sold for $2 each or 6 for $10 (A portion of the proceeds goes to the American Cancer Society / Relay for Life).
Contact Information: (850) 492-0611, info@florabama.com, http://www.florabama.com/Special%20Events/Chili%20Cook%20Off/chilibowl.htm, Alternative contact: (251) 980-5116
Description: Chili cook-off benefiting the American Cancer Society. Cash prizes and people's choice award. Live music.

FIREFIGHT AT SPANISH SPRINGS

City/County/Region: The Villages / Orange / Central
Location: Town Square of The Villages of Spanish Springs and Market Square at Lake Sumter Landing (2 simultaneous locations)
General Date: 1st Saturday in February
Duration: 1 day
Year Started: 1997
Approx. Attendance: 15,000
Public Admission Fee: Free
Other Fees/Costs: Contest entry fee is $100 (tax deductible contribution).
Contact Information: (352) 751-6700, info@thevillages.com, http://www.thevillages.com, Alternative contact: (352) 753-8505, (800) 245-1081
Description: Chili cook-off benefiting the Rotary Club of the Villages Foundation, Inc.'s community projects. Over 50 chili teams compete for cash prizes, best-themed booth, and people's choice chili. Event also features many vendors, clowns, and live entertainment.

TITUSVILLE SUNRISE ROTARY CLUB CHILI COOKOFF

City/County/Region: Titusville / Brevard / Central East
Location: US 1 (between Julia Street and Main Street) on the west end of Main Street
General Date: 1st Saturday in February
Duration: 1 day
Year Started: 2004
Approx. Attendance: Varies
Public Admission Fee: Unknown
Other Fees/Costs: Contest entry fee is $20.

3 - Carnivore's Delight

Contact Information: (321) 264-0518, twomenes@bellsouth.net, http://www.nbbd.com/StreetParty/index.html, Alternative contact: Titusville Area Chamber of Commerce, (321) 267-3036, johnson@titusville.org

Description: More than 60 of the best chili chefs around competing for "fame and fortune" (cash, trophy and a certificate). All proceeds benefit the "Up to Present" program of the North Brevard Sharing Center. Hosted by Titusville Rotary Clubs and held during the Downtown Titusville Street Party.

'SMOKE ON THE WATER' BBQ ~ *Great for Kids!*

City/County/Region: Winter Haven / Polk / Central
Location: 2400 Havendale Blvd.
General Date: 2nd weekend in February
Duration: 2 days
Year Started: 2005
Approx. Attendance: 5,000
Public Admission Fee: Unknown
Other Fees/Costs: Contest entry fee is $75 per category for Pro division, $25 per category for Backyard division.
Contact Information: (863) 287-3075, froglips02@aol.com, http://boysandgirlsbbq.com
Description: Citrus Center Boys & Girls Club BBQ competition. This contest has both a Pro division and a Backyard division contest, drawing some of the best BBQ teams in the country and the top teams in the state. Florida BBQ Association (FBA) sanctioned BBQ competition and qualifier for the Jack Daniels

World BBQ Championship. Runs two days for the competitors, one day for the public. Other activities include an interactive children's area, seaplane rides, and live musical entertainment.

CHILI IN THE VILLAGE REGIONAL COOKOFF

City/County/Region: Pinecrest / Miami-Dade / Southeast
Location: Pinecrest Gardens
General Date: 2nd Saturday in February
Duration: 1 day
Year Started: Unavailable
Approx. Attendance: Varies
Public Admission Fee: Unknown
Other Fees/Costs: Contest entry fee is $25 for International Chili Society (ICS) members, $67 for non-members.
Contact Information: (305) 669-6942, mgilbert@pinecrest-fl.gov, http://www.pinecrestgardens.com
Description: Chili cook-off with red chili, chili verde, and salsa categories.

PLANT CITY ARTS COUNCIL CHILI COOKOFF

City/County/Region: Plant City / Hillsborough / Central West
Location: Historic Plant City Train Depot
General Date: 2nd Saturday in February
Duration: 1 day
Year Started: 1991
Approx. Attendance: 400
Public Admission Fee: Free
Other Fees/Costs: $5 charge for tastes.
Contact Information: (813) 757-9110, barbaramoore24@tampabay.rr.com, http://www.plantcityartscouncil.com

Description: Chili cook-off benefiting the Plant City Arts Council. Chefs compete for cash prizes in three categories—mild, spicy, novelty. The public can taste entries and vote for the "People's Choice" award (nominal charge for tastes). Live entertainment includes dancers, singers, and music.

Florida Keys Regional Cookoff

City/County/Region: Key Largo / Monroe / Southwest
Location: Rowell's Marine, MM 104.5 Bayside
General Date: 2nd Sunday in February
Duration: 1 day
Year Started: Unavailable
Approx. Attendance: Varies
Public Admission Fee: Unknown
Other Fees/Costs: Contest entry fee for chili is $35 for ICS members, $77 for non-members. Entry fees for Verde $15, Salsa $10.
Contact Information: (786) 423-4537, whitney@homesteadgas.com
Description: Chili cook-off benefiting the Key Largo Rotary Club Charity Events Fund. Red, verde, and salsa categories.

Estero High Key Club Chili Cookoff

City/County/Region: Estero / Lee / Southwest
Location: Three Oaks Community Park
General Date: Last Saturday in February
Duration: 1 day
Year Started: 2003
Approx. Attendance: Varies

Public Admission Fee: Unknown
Other Fees/Costs: Contest entry fee is $25.
Contact Information: (941) 947-9400, JADFCS@aol.com, Alternative contact: Janad@leeschools.net
Description: Chili cook-off benefiting Key Club Activities. "Cooks" parade, live entertainment. Estero High Key Club sells other food including cornbread, soda, and hotdogs.

Top Of The Lake BBQ Affair

City/County/Region: Okeechobee / Okeechobee / Central East
Location: American Legion Fair Grounds
General Date: Last weekend in February or 1st weekend in March
Duration: 2 days
Year Started: 2003
Approx. Attendance: 2,000
Public Admission Fee: Free
Other Fees/Costs: BBQ lunch and dinner tickets on sale in advance at the Okeechobee Main Street office or by calling phone number below.
Contact Information: (863) 357-6246, ljwilliams@ mainstreetokeechobee.com, http://www.mainstreetokeechobee.com
Description: Barbecue cook-off sponsored by Okeechobee Main Street. BBQ Lunch and Dinners. Live music.

Gulf Coast Regional Chili Cookoff

City/County/Region: Eastpoint / Franklin / Northwest
Location: St. George Island

3 - Carnivore's Delight

General Date:	1st Saturday in March
Duration:	1 day
Year Started:	1983
Approx. Attendance:	Varies
Public Admission Fee:	Free
Other Fees/Costs:	Contest entry fee is $40 for International Chili Society (ICS) members, $82 for non-members. After judging, samples are sold for $1 a bowl.
Contact Information:	(850) 653-6718, grayshep@yahoo.com
Description:	Chili competition benefiting St. George Island Volunteer Fire Department and sanctioned by the International Chili Society. After judging, the competition chilis are sold at a nominal charge per bowl. Competitors often cook other items (e.g., chili, barbecue, hamburgers, etc.) for sale as long as 100% of the proceeds are donated to the fire department. Participants may dress in costume or decorate their booths. The fire department has food booths selling BBQ, fried oysters, and chili served in bread bowls. In addition to the food, there is an auction, a Mr. and Mrs. Chili Pepper competition, and a crock-pot chili competition open to everyone. Morning starts with a 5K Run.

PIG ON THE POND - *Great for Kids!*

City/County/Region:	Clermont / Lake / Central
Location:	Clermont Waterfront Park on Lake Minneola
General Date:	2nd weekend in March
Duration:	3 days
Year Started:	Unavailable
Approx. Attendance:	20,000

Public Admission Fee: $

Other Fees/Costs: Admission is $2, free parking and shuttle rides are included. Tickets $12 for Friday night's concert. "Pig Bucks" required to purchase at "BBQ Alley" or pay $5 to sample the barbecue and choose your own winner in the People's Choice contest.

Contact Information: (352) 516-7771, biddlerosie@aol.com, http://www.pigonthepond.org

Description: Two-day celebration of community. Nationally sanctioned BBQ cookoff, the Great Chili Challenge, food-eating contests, People's choice BBQ tasting, dessert bake-off. Midway carnival, major and local entertainment, various games and contests (like the Tickle Pig contest where persons or businesses decorate porta-potties), arts and crafts, and more! Unique event raises funds for educational and scholarship programs in South Lake County.

ASTOR CHAMBER OF COMMERCE CHILI COOK-OFF

City/County/Region: Astor / Lake / Central

Location: Blackwater Inn Restaurant by the Astor Bridge on the banks of the St. John's River

General Date: 2nd Saturday in March

Duration: 1 day

Year Started: 2006

Approx. Attendance: Varies

Public Admission Fee: Free

Other Fees/Costs: Contest registration fee is $25, after March 1st, registration fee is $40. If you want to

3 - Carnivore's Delight

Contact Information: participant in tasting for the People's Choice category, the cost is $5 per person.
(352) 759-3422, lhillinpierson@netzero.com, http://www.astorchamber.com/chile_cookoff.html, Alternative contact: homes@totcon.com, (352) 759-2496

Description: Anyone can enter the contest (fee required). Two categories—Red Chili (no beans) with blind judging by area judges and the People's Choice (with beans). Also award for the best booth display. All 1st place winners receive cash and trophies. Vendors located around the contestants, featuring arts, crafts, flea markets, boiled peanuts, ice cream, and more! DJ provides music for listening and dancing. Hosted by the Astor Area Chamber of Commerce.

CACTUS JACK'S CHILI COOKOFF

City/County/Region: Salt Springs / Marion / Central
Location: Cactus Jack's, 23740 NE CR 314
General Date: Every March
Duration: 1 day
Year Started: Unavailable
Approx. Attendance: Varies
Public Admission Fee: Unknown
Other Fees/Costs: Contest entry fee is $20.
Contact Information: (352) 685-2244
Description: Chili cook-off benefiting the Salt Springs Civic Association.

NAPLES COUNTRY JAM CHILI COOKOFF

City/County/Region: Naples / Collier / Southwest
Location: Vineyards Community Park, 6231 Arbor Blvd.
General Date: 2nd Saturday in March
Duration: 1 day
Year Started: 2001
Approx. Attendance: Varies
Public Admission Fee: $$
Other Fees/Costs: Must pay admission to the Country Jam. $15 (per day) advance purchase, $20 (per day) at the gate. Children 10 and under free. Contest entry fees are $35 for chili, $10 for salsa.
Contact Information: (239) 434-9888, info@countryjamnaples.com, http://www.countryjamnaples.com, Alternative contact: Collier County Parks and Recreation Department, (239) 353-0404
Description: Chili cook-off and salsa competition. The cook-off is held in conjunction with Country Jam which is organized by the Collier County Parks and Recreation Department. The Country Jam is always the second weekend in March with the cook-off on Saturday.

BLUEGRASS & BBQ FESTIVAL

City/County/Region: Auburndale / Polk / Central
Location: Market World - 1052 Highway 92W
General Date: 3rd weekend in March
Duration: 4 days
Year Started: 1993
Approx. Attendance: Varies
Public Admission Fee: Unknown
Other Fees/Costs: Unavailable

Contact Information: (863) 665-0062, info@intlmarketworld.com, http://www.intlmarketworld.com/ev_blue.html

Description: Wide variety of barbecue and other food, live bluegrass music, cloggers, dueling banjos contest. Vendors, Buffalo farm on site, vendors, large flea market next door. Dry camping for over 200 RVs. Some electric and water available.

BEULAH SAUSAGE FESTIVAL ~ *Great for Kids!*

City/County/Region: Pensacola / Escambia / Northwest
Location: Across the street from the Beulah Fire Dept
General Date: 3rd weekend in March
Duration: 3 days
Year Started: 1987
Approx. Attendance: 40,000
Public Admission Fee: $
Other Fees/Costs: Admission is $5 per person per day which includes all shows for that day. Kids 11 and under free. Admission does not include parking. This is handled by private groups and individuals. Average parking cost is $2.
Contact Information: (850) 944-3167, question@beulahsausagefest.com, http://www.beulahsausagefest.com
Description: The Beulah Fire Department holds this annual sausage festival to raise funds in support of community fire protection. Features live country music, arts and crafts booths, carnival-style rides, games, and, of course, lots of sausage! No coolers or pets. Bring lawn chairs or a blanket to sit on.

CHILI BLAZE

City/County/Region:	Pinellas Park / Pinellas / Central West
Location:	Firefighter's Field, 5000 81st St. No Pinellas Park FL (behind Station 33)
General Date:	3rd Friday night in March
Duration:	1 day
Year Started:	2000
Approx. Attendance:	12,500
Public Admission Fee:	$
Other Fees/Costs:	Wristband for $7 includes all chili samples. Contest entry fee $25 for professional category.
Contact Information:	(727) 541-0713, info@chiliblaze.com, http://www.chiliblaze.com, Alternative contact: 727-687-4494
Description:	Chili cook-off hosted by the Pinellas Park Firefighters, IAFF Local 2193, benefiting MDA. Other activities include a chili dog eating contest, bike show, and live music entertainment.

BACKYARD BBQ BLAST

City/County/Region:	Jacksonville / Duval / Northeast
Location:	Jacksonville
General Date:	Last weekend in March
Duration:	3 days
Year Started:	2006
Approx. Attendance:	Varies
Public Admission Fee:	$$
Other Fees/Costs:	Daily admission $20 available at the gate, Ticketmaster, Jiffy Lube, and Johnson's Family Flea Market. Contest entry fee $60 per category, $25 per Backyard category.

3 - Carnivore's Delight

Contact Information: (904) 742-6720, johnsonfleamrkt@aol.com, http://www.jacksonvillebbqblast.com
Description: Barbecue cook-off with live music and lots of activities—paintball, battle of the bands, fishing tournament, bike ride and raffle.

DENNING'S LOUNGE CHILI COOKOFF

City/County/Region: Tampa / Hillsborough / Central West
Location: Denning's Lounge, 13606 N. Florida Ave.
General Date: 3rd Saturday in March
Duration: 1 day
Year Started: 2002
Approx. Attendance: Varies
Public Admission Fee: Unknown
Other Fees/Costs: Contest entry fee is $30.
Contact Information: (813) 961-7300
Description: Chili cook-off benefiting Bay Area Firefighters Inc. and Make-A-Wish Foundation.

ENGLEWOOD BEACH / BURR SMIDT MEMORIAL CHILI COOKOFF

City/County/Region: Englewood / Sarasota / Central West
Location: Chadwick Park on Manasota Key
General Date: Last Saturday in March
Duration: 1 day
Year Started: 2002
Approx. Attendance: Varies
Public Admission Fee: Free
Other Fees/Costs: Contest entry fee is $20.
Contact Information: (941) 587-1608, drsaunders26@msn.com, Alternative contact: (941) 266-3799
Description: Chili cook-off benefiting a local organization.

Florida Sunshine Pod Cookoff

City/County/Region:	Englewood / Sarasota / Central West
Location:	Chadwick Park on Manasota Key
General Date:	Last Sunday in March
Duration:	1 day
Year Started:	2002
Approx. Attendance:	Varies
Public Admission Fee:	Free
Other Fees/Costs:	Contest entry fee is $20.
Contact Information:	(941) 266-3799, drsaunders26@msn.com, Alternative contact: (941) 587-1608
Description:	Chili cook-off (chili grind only) benefiting a local charity.

Hog Wild and Pig Crazy Barbecue Cook-off ~ *Great for Kids!*

City/County/Region:	Lake City / Columbia / North Central
Location:	Memorial Stadium in downtown Lake City
General Date:	1st Friday and Saturday in April
Duration:	2 days
Year Started:	1993
Approx. Attendance:	6,000
Public Admission Fee:	Free
Other Fees/Costs:	Unavailable
Contact Information:	(386) 758-5448, hogwildbbq@yahoo.com
Description:	Sponsored by the Lake City-Columbia County Parks and Recreation Department and is sanctioned by the Sanctioned Contest Network. Categories include chicken, ribs, pork, brisket,

sauce, dessert, wings, kid's group. In addition to the cook-off, the event includes craft booths and carnival rides. Local dance and singing groups offer live entertainment throughout the event.

'Make it Mild or Make it Wild' Chili Cook-off ~ *Great for Kids!*

City/County/Region:	Jacksonville / Duval / Northeast
Location:	Kathryn Abbey Hanna Park
General Date:	1st Saturday in April
Duration:	1 day
Year Started:	1999
Approx. Attendance:	Varies
Public Admission Fee:	Free
Other Fees/Costs:	Contest entry fee is $30.
Contact Information:	(904) 880-2490, chilicookoff2006@bellsouth.net, http://www.clarkeschool.org/content/news/chili2.pdf
Description:	Chili cook-off (awards for hottest, most unique, best overall, and people's choice) benefiting the Clarke Jacksonville Auditory/Oral Center, a nonprofit organization that teaches hearing impaired children to listen and speak for themselves. Raffles throughout the day, silent auction, live bands. Kid's activities and food include a huge slide, popcorn, cotton candy, snow cones, hot dogs and drinks.

Celebrate Bonita District Chili Cookoff

City/County/Region: Bonita Springs / Lee / Southwest
Location: Old US 41 Depot Park
General Date: In April
Duration: 1 day
Year Started: Unavailable
Approx. Attendance: Varies
Public Admission Fee: Unknown
Other Fees/Costs: Contest entry fee is $35 for International Chili Society (ICS) members, $77 for non-members.
Contact Information: (239) 949-7525, SRSeacat@aol.com
Description: Chili cook-off benefiting the Bonita Springs Assistance Office.

Boggy Barbecue Cookoff

City/County/Region: Niceville / Okaloosa / Northwest
Location: Parking lot of The Pavilion (Assisted Living Facility), Hwy 20 in downtown Niceville.
General Date: 2nd Saturday in April
Duration: 2 days
Year Started: 2006
Approx. Attendance: Varies
Public Admission Fee: Unknown
Other Fees/Costs: Contest entry fee is $60 per category for Professional division, $25 per category for Backyard division.
Contact Information: (850) 897-2728, boggybbq@cox.net, http://members.cox.net/boggybbq/index.htm
Description: Barbecue cook-off benefiting a local charity. Both a Professional and Backyard Division! Charity may rotate each year and location may move from year to year.

Rhythm and Ribs Festival ~ *Great for Kids!*

City/County/Region: St. Augustine / St. Johns / Northeast
Location: Francis Field at US1 on Castillo Drive
General Date: 2nd weekend in April
Duration: 3 days
Year Started: Unavailable
Approx. Attendance: Varies
Public Admission Fee: Free
Other Fees/Costs: Unavailable
Contact Information: (904) 797-7924, event@rhythmandribs.net, http://www.rhythmandribs.net
Description: Stomp your feet and smack your lips at this annual festival featuring championship BBQ dishes from around the country. A variety of entertainment throughout the weekend. Lots of children's activities. This festival is sponsored by the St. Augustine Sunrise Rotary Club. Proceeds will be used to fund community and international charitable projects.

Spring Jubilee Chili Cook-off ~ *Great for Kids!*

City/County/Region: Riverview / Hillsborough / Central West
Location: 10428 Saint Stephen Circle
General Date: In April
Duration: 1 day
Year Started: 2002
Approx. Attendance: Varies
Public Admission Fee: Free
Other Fees/Costs: Contest entry fee is $50 for 3-person team, $75 for 3-person "Professional" team, and $250 for "Corporate Corner" team. Sample cups are $5 each to the public.

Contact Information: (813) 217-1095, info@springjubilee.com, http://www.springjubilee.com, Alternative contact: (813) 789-9912

Description: Chili cook-off benefiting All Children's Hospital. The cook-off is held in conjunction with the Spring Jubilee celebration. Other Spring Jubilee activities include midway rides (must purchase tickets), live entertainment, car show, and fireworks.

DeLand Wild Game Feast

City/County/Region: De Land / Volusia / Central East
Location: The Tommy Lawrence Arena at the Volusia County Fair Grounds
General Date: 1st Thursday in May
Duration: 1 day
Year Started: 1992
Approx. Attendance: Varies
Public Admission Fee: $$$
Other Fees/Costs: Tickets are $50.
Contact Information: (386) 738-0649, contact@delandbreakfastrotary.org, http://www.delandbreakfastrotary.org/events2.htm
Description: A sampling of domestic and wild game dishes. Proceeds from this event are shared with local nonprofit organizations.

Battle of the Badges – *Great for Kids!*

City/County/Region: Largo / Pinellas / Central West
Location: Largo Central Park
General Date: 1st Saturday in May
Duration: 1 day

3 - Carnivore's Delight

Year Started:	Unavailable
Approx. Attendance:	Varies
Public Admission Fee:	Free
Other Fees/Costs:	Attendees asked to pay a donation for tickets to sample the chili and ribs. Wristbands and tickets sold for some of the children's activities.
Contact Information:	(727) 742-2380, badges2006@yahoo.com, http://www.chiliandribs.com
Description:	Chili and rib cook-off between police officers and firefighters within Pinellas County. Also features music, games, entertainment, and vendors. Many free family activities, but wristbands and tickets are sold for some of the children's activities (interactive inflatable games—bounce house, obstacle course, giant slide, etc). Event is a fundraiser for Mothers Against Drunk Driving (MADD) and Removing Intoxicated Drivers (RID) and is presented by Carey, Leisure & Magazine, Attorneys at Law.

SMOKE 'N BLUES BBQ - *Great for Kids!*

City/County/Region:	St. Cloud / Osceola / Central
Location:	Veteran's Park, Downtown St. Cloud
General Date:	2nd weekend in May
Duration:	2 days
Year Started:	2003
Approx. Attendance:	3,000
Public Admission Fee:	Free
Other Fees/Costs:	Unavailable
Contact Information:	(407) 498-0008, http://www.stcloudmainstreetflorida.org

Description: BBQ competition featuring Florida's Best Masters of the Barbeque. Also features live Blues music and a Wine Tasting Tent. Florida BBQ Association sanctioned competition for both pros and backyard teams. Festivities include crafters, kids play area, BBQ vendors and much more.

BBQ<small>FEST</small> ~ *Great for Kids!*

City/County/Region: Tampa / Hillsborough / Central West
Location: Curtis Hixon Park
General Date: Last weekend in May
Duration: 3 days
Year Started: 2004
Approx. Attendance: Varies
Public Admission Fee: $
Other Fees/Costs: General admission is $15 per day, or $30 Friday and $40 Saturday-Sunday reserved seating. Under 12 free with paid adult.
Contact Information: (813) 786-6878, BBQfest@aol.com, http://www.bbqfest.net
Description: BBQ lovers paradise including BBQ rib cook-off, music featuring blues, classic rock and country, classic car show, motorcycle show, and lots of kids activities. Some proceeds go to charity.

I<small>NDIAN</small> R<small>IVER</small> C<small>OUNTY</small> F<small>IREFIGHTERS</small>' C<small>HILI</small> C<small>OOKOFF</small> ~ *Great for Kids!*

City/County/Region: Vero Beach / Indian River / Central East
Location: 3001 Ocean Drive at Humiston Park

General Date: Saturday of Memorial Day weekend
Duration: 1 day
Year Started: 2004
Approx. Attendance: 6,000
Public Admission Fee: Free
Other Fees/Costs: Wristbands sold for unlimited chili tasting for $6 and unlimited Kid's Bounce Houses for $5.
Contact Information: (772) 567-2201, ircffa@aol.com, http://www.IAFF2201.org
Description: Chili cook-off and tasting, hot-wing eating contest, hot dog eating contest, jalapeno pepper plant contest, concert, kid's Bounce House, face painting. Proceeds benefit the Community Child Care Resources of Indian River County.

Sun-N-Fun RV Resort Chili Cookoff

City/County/Region: Sarasota / Sarasota / Central West
Location: Sun-N-Fun RV Resort, 7125 Fruitville Rd.
General Date: 3rd weekend in September
Duration: 2 days
Year Started: Unavailable
Approx. Attendance: Varies
Public Admission Fee: Unknown
Other Fees/Costs: Contest entry fee is $20.
Contact Information: (800) 843-2421, jholback@sunnfunfl.com, http://www.sunnfunfl.com
Description: Chili cook-off benefits local charity. Live music and car show.

Florida Barbecue Association Funcook ~ *Great for Kids!*

City/County/Region: Crystal River / Citrus / Central West
Location: Lake Rousseau RV Park
General Date: Labor Day weekend
Duration: 2 days
Year Started: 2000
Approx. Attendance: Varies
Public Admission Fee: Unknown
Other Fees/Costs: Unavailable
Contact Information: (352) 795-6336, chuck@flbbq.org, http://www.flbbq.org/funcook_agenda.htm, Alternative contact: http://www.lakerousseaurvpark.com, info@lakerousseaurvpark.com
Description: Judging of barbecue dishes—chicken, ribs, pork, brisket. Separate category for kids (chicken and burgers).

Q-Fest BBQ & Music Festival ~ *Great for Kids!*

City/County/Region: Grant / Brevard / Central East
Location: 4580 1st Street
General Date: 4th Saturday in September
Duration: 1 day
Year Started: 2002
Approx. Attendance: 18,000
Public Admission Fee: Free
Other Fees/Costs: Free parking.
Contact Information: (321) 952-4938, rtibbitts@mindspring.com, http://www.q-fest.com
Description: KCBS sanctioned barbecue competition (chicken, ribs, pork, brisket categories) with cash prizes. Also a kids contest. Live music, arts and crafts, 5K Run. Proceeds benefit Toyz 4 Kidz.

MINNEOLA FALL FEST BBQ CONTEST

City/County/Region: Minneola / Lake / Central
Location: Minneola
General Date: Last weekend in October
Duration: 2 days
Year Started: Unavailable
Approx. Attendance: Varies
Public Admission Fee: Unknown
Other Fees/Costs: Contest entry fee is $75 per category (chicken, ribs, pork, brisket).
Contact Information: (352) 536-1719, eventsunlimited@cfl.rr.com, http://www.ci.minneola.fl.us/recreation.html, Alternative contact: City of Minneola Recreation Department, (352) 394-3598, x 27
Description: This contest is usually the FBA Florida State Championship. Takes place in conjunction with Minneola's fall festival.

MULBERRY FINE SWINE AT THE PIT

City/County/Region: Mulberry / Polk / Central
Location: Mulberry
General Date: 1st weekend in October
Duration: 2 days
Year Started: Unavailable
Approx. Attendance: Varies
Public Admission Fee: Unknown
Other Fees/Costs: Contest entry fee is $60 for Professional division, $30 for Backyard division.
Contact Information: (863) 293-4141, citymanager@eaglelake-fla.com, http://www.eaglelake-fla.com, Alternative contact: (863) 559-2409
Description: Barbecue competition (chicken, ribs, pork, brisket, and overall categories).

Hernando County BBQ & Rodeo Festival ~ *Great for Kids!*

City/County/Region:	Brooksville / Hernando / Central West
Location:	Hernando County Airport
General Date:	2nd weekend in October
Duration:	3 days
Year Started:	1977
Approx. Attendance:	15,000
Public Admission Fee:	$
Other Fees/Costs:	Tickets are $12 in advance and $14 at the gate for adults, and $5 in advance and $6 at the gate for children. Children younger than 3 are admitted for free.
Contact Information:	(352) 796-2290, info@hernandocattlemen.com, http://www.hernandocattlemen.com/index.html
Description:	KCBS Sanctioned BBQ Championship Cook-off. Event also features three rodeos, Country Music concerts, carnival, and vendors. Partial proceeds from the Festival benefit the Egypt Shrine Hospital Transportation Fund, Hernando-Central and Brooksville Sr. FFA Chapter, Hernando County Sheriff's Explorers, Pasco-Hernando Community College Academy of Law Enforcement, and Hernando County's Youth In Agriculture.

Marion County Chili Cook-Off ~ *Great for Kids!*

City/County/Region:	Ocala / Marion / Central
Location:	Southeastern Livestock Pavilion located on North East Jacksonville Road
General Date:	2nd or 3rd Saturday in October
Duration:	1 day
Year Started:	1982
Approx. Attendance:	5,000

Public Admission Fee: $

Other Fees/Costs: Admission fee is $3 for adults, $2 for senior citizens, $2 for students with an ID, and $1 for children 12 and under. Chili sold for 25 cents for a sampler cup, 75 cents for a 4-ounce cup. Chili contest entry fee is $45 if registered by September 1; $50 if registered by October 1; and $60 after that.

Contact Information: (352) 867-6929, info@CS-Ocala.org, http://www.cs-ocala.org/chili, Phone number is usually not in operation until the middle of August.

Description: Teams throughout Marion County compete for the title of Best Chili in Marion County. Various divisions winners and a People's Choice Award for the best chili voted on by the public. Also a salsa and cake competition. Sampling of the chili and other food available. Music entertainment all day and a children's area.

SOUTHEAST CHILI COOKOFF

City/County/Region: Homosassa / Citrus / Central West

Location: Nature's RV Campground & Resort, 10359 W. Halls River Rd.

General Date: 2nd Saturday in October

Duration: 1 day

Year Started: 2000

Approx. Attendance: Varies

Public Admission Fee: Unknown

Other Fees/Costs: Contest entry fee is $20.

Contact Information: (210) 887-8827, chiliflorida@aol.com, Alternative contact: Nature's RV Campground & Resort, (352) 628-9544

Description: Chili cook-off benefiting Rotary Club Charities.

Food Fest! Your Complete Guide to Florida's Food Festivals

WATERFRONT CHILI COOKOFF

City/County/Region:	Homosassa / Citrus / Central West
Location:	Nature's RV Campground & Resort, 10359 W. Halls River Rd.
General Date:	2nd Sunday in October
Duration:	1 day
Year Started:	Unavailable
Approx. Attendance:	Varies
Public Admission Fee:	Unknown
Other Fees/Costs:	Contest entry fee is $15.
Contact Information:	(210) 887-8827, chiliflorida@aol.com, Alternative contact: Nature's RV Campground & Resort, (352) 628-9544
Description:	Chili cook-off benefiting local charity.

BELLEVIEW CHILI COOK-OFF ~ *Great for Kids!*

City/County/Region:	Belleview / Marion / Central
Location:	Market of Marion
General Date:	3rd Saturday in October
Duration:	1 day
Year Started:	2005
Approx. Attendance:	2,500
Public Admission Fee:	Free
Other Fees/Costs:	Contest entry fee is $50. Wristband must be purchased to sample chili.
Contact Information:	(352) 307-7306, http://www.belleviewchilicookoff.com, Alternative contact: (352) 425-0417
Description:	Chili cook-off benefiting Junior Acheivement of Marion County. Kids activities, raffle, musical entertainment.

Great Bowls of Fire Chili Cookoff

City/County/Region: De Land / Volusia / Central East
Location: Downtown Main Street
General Date: 3rd Saturday in October
Duration: 1 day
Year Started: Unavailable
Approx. Attendance: Varies
Public Admission Fee: Unknown
Other Fees/Costs: Contest entry fee is $25.
Contact Information: (386) 740-6813, delandhouse@msn.com, http://www.delandhouse.com
Description: Chili cook-off benefiting the West Volusia Historical Society and DeLand Downtown Rotary Club.

Hospice Chili Cookoff

City/County/Region: Wilton Manors / Broward / Southeast
Location: Big Dog Saloon
General Date: 3rd or 4th Saturday in October
Duration: 1 day
Year Started: 1995
Approx. Attendance: 3,000
Public Admission Fee: Free
Other Fees/Costs: Contest entry fee $45.
Contact Information: (954) 561-4304, Wwwbigdogsaloon@aol.com, http://www.hospicecareflorida.org/events-chili.html, Alternative contact: (954) 467-7423
Description: Chili cook-off benefiting HospiceCare of Southeast Florida and sponsored by Big Dog Saloon. Charity raffle, music, trophy presentation.

Leesburg Chili Cook-Off

City/County/Region: Leesburg / Lake / Central
Location: Towne Square, Downtown Leesburg
General Date: Saturday in late October or early November
Duration: 1 day
Year Started: 2000
Approx. Attendance: Varies
Public Admission Fee: Unknown
Other Fees/Costs: Contest entry fee is $85 plus extra for table and tent rental.
Contact Information: (352) 326-8090, info@downtownleesburgfl.com, http://www.downtownleesburgfl.com
Description: Chili cook-off competition, live entertainment, beer and wine. Presented by the Leesburg Downtown Business Association.

Palm Beach County Firefighters/Paramedics M.D.A. Chili Cookoff

City/County/Region: Lake Worth / Palm Beach / Southeast
Location: Sound Advice Amphitheatre at the South Florida Fairgrounds
General Date: 3rd Saturday in November
Duration: 1 day
Year Started: 1997
Approx. Attendance: Varies
Public Admission Fee: Unknown
Other Fees/Costs: No contest entry fee other than 5 gallons of chili.
Contact Information: (561) 436-4724, sparky1783@adelphia.net, http://www.iaff2928.com
Description: Chili cook-off benefiting the Muscular Dystrophy Association.

3 - Carnivore's Delight

First Coast Ham Jam ~ *Great for Kids!*

City/County/Region: Green Cove Springs / Clay / Northeast
Location: Reynolds Park Yacht Center, 1063 Bulkhead Road
General Date: 1st weekend in November
Duration: 4 days
Year Started: 1988
Approx. Attendance: 30,000
Public Admission Fee: $$
Other Fees/Costs: Tickets Thursday and Sunday $11, Friday and Saturday $22. Parking fee is charged.
Contact Information: (904) 276-4746, munsey69@comcast.net, http://www.hamjam.org, Alternative contact: (904) 838-5530
Description: Florida's Official BBQ Cooking Contest. Annual event sanctioned by the Florida BarBQue Association. Features concerts by national country artists, exhibits, rides, arts and crafts.

Ribfest ~ *Great for Kids!*

City/County/Region: St. Petersburg / Pinellas / Central West
Location: Vinoy Park, Fifth Avenue NE and Bayshore Drive
General Date: 2nd weekend in November
Duration: 3 days
Year Started: 1989
Approx. Attendance: 35,000
Public Admission Fee: $
Other Fees/Costs: Admission is $6 per day in advance at Ticketmaster plus service charges, or $10 at the gate (no re-entry). Ages 12 and younger are free.

Contact Information: (727) 528-3828, asayler@tampabay.rr.com, http://www.ribfest.org

Description: In addition to the ribs, there's lots of other activities including classic rock concerts, Corvette car show, Harley Davidson show, children's entertainment area with games for kids, and of course, the best ribs in the world! Ribfest is a charity fund raiser, with all proceeds going to All Children's Hospital, child abuse prevention programs, college scholarships and other children-related charities.

PLANT CITY PIG JAM ~ *Great for Kids!*

City/County/Region: Plant City / Hillsborough / Central West

Location: Randy Larson Softball Four-Plex, 1900 South Park Rd & 1401 Albertsons Drive

General Date: 3rd Saturday in November

Duration: 1 day

Year Started: 2003

Approx. Attendance: 6,000

Public Admission Fee: Free

Other Fees/Costs: Parking is $3.

Contact Information: (813) 754-3707, info@plantcity.org, http://www.plantcity.org, Alternative contact: http://www.plantcitychamber.org, http://isctest.home.att.net/home.htm, (800) 760-2315

Description: Finger-licking good barbecue, live entertainment, children's activities. This event is sanctioned by the Kansas City Barbeque Society and contestants participate in three classes—Professional, Amateur, and Kids.

BEEFCEMBER FEST

City/County/Region: Starke / Bradford / North Central
Location: Starke
General Date: 2nd weekend in December
Duration: 2 days
Year Started: 1986
Approx. Attendance: Varies
Public Admission Fee: Unknown
Other Fees/Costs: Unavailable
Contact Information: (904) 226-5027, justinm@nodarse.com, Alternative contact: jess32091@yahoo.com
Description: Barbecue cook-off (formerly called the Antique Engine Cookoff).

4   Fruit Medley

Any good doctor worth his apple should prescribe his patients one of these festivals. The food festivals listed in this chapter feature citrus and a wide variety of other fruits. What better or more fun way to get your Vitamin C?

The citrus industry is an integral part of Florida's economy. Each year Florida is the nation's top producer of citrus—oranges are the number one crop and most grapefruit distributed in the United States is grown in Florida. Florida citrus varieties range from grapefruit, oranges, tangerines, tangelos (a cross between a tangerine and a grapefruit), mandarins, lemons, limes and kumquats. Kumquats are the smallest of the citrus fruits, with a thick edible rind. Oval ones tend to be sweet and oblong ones tart. Try them both, but definitely try the kumquat pie! The USDA food pyramid recommends 2-4 servings of fruit daily—hopefully the festivals listed below will help you meet that quota!

Look Mom, no hands!

Florida Citrus Festival -- *Great for Kids!*

City/County/Region: Winter Haven / Polk / Central
Location: 100 Cypress Gardens Blvd SW
General Date: Begins last Thursday in January
Duration: 11 days
Year Started: 1924
Approx. Attendance: 160,000
Public Admission Fee: $
Other Fees/Costs: Gate admission $7. Younger than age 3 free. Ride pass $16 (all ages).
Contact Information: (863) 292-9810, michelle@citrusfestival.com, http://www.citrusfestival.com
Description: Celebrate citrus! Various competitions such as the grapefruit packing, hay bale decorating, photography, and many more. Miss Florida Citrus pageant. Livestock for show and sale. Parade, carnival rides, and other entertainment.

Kumquat Festival -- *Great for Kids!*

City/County/Region: Dade City / Pasco / Central West
Location: Historic downtown, 7th Street and Meridian
General Date: Last Saturday in January
Duration: 1 day
Year Started: 1998
Approx. Attendance: 35,000
Public Admission Fee: Free
Other Fees/Costs: Unavailable
Contact Information: (352) 567-3769, info@dadecitychamber.org, http://www.kumquatfestival.com
Description: This festival serves up an assortment of kumquat goodies including the famous Kumquat pie. Over 300 craft and food vendors,

4 stages with local entertainment performing throughout the day, antique car show, children's section, and animal world. Interesting activities for all ages! Many pre-festival events take place the week leading up to the festival beginning on the Saturday before the festival. These activities include a Kumquat Beauty Pageant, recipe contest, quilt challenge contest, window decorating contest, and an open house at the Kumquat Grower's ending with a 4H Dinner and children's parade. The festival itself opens the last Saturday morning in January with a 5K run.

Sour Orange Festival

City/County/Region: Lakeport / Glades / Southwest
Location: Lakeport Community Center, 10245 Red Barn Road, NW
General Date: 2nd Saturday in February
Duration: 1 day
Year Started: 1994
Approx. Attendance: Varies
Public Admission Fee: Unknown
Other Fees/Costs: Unavailable
Contact Information: (863) 946-0300, info@gladescountyedc.com, www.gladescountyedc.com, Alternative Contact: Glades County Chamber of Commerce, http://www.gladesonline.com, gccommerce@gladesonline.com, (863) 946-0440
Description: Oranges, sour orange pie, pie-eating contest, live music, and cook-off. Craft booths selling handmade crafts, T-shirts, sweatshirts, the famous Sour Orange Cook Book, and of course, sour orange entrees and desserts.

FLORIDA STRAWBERRY FESTIVAL ~ *Great for Kids!*

City/County/Region:	Plant City / Hillsborough / Central West
Location:	Plant City Fairgrounds, 2202 West Reynolds Street
General Date:	Begins 1st weekend in March
Duration:	11 days
Year Started:	1930
Approx. Attendance:	550,000
Public Admission Fee:	$
Other Fees/Costs:	Advanced gate admission is $8 (for ages 13 & up) if purchased on or before March 1 or $9 if purchased at the gate. Advanced youth gate admission is (for ages 6-12) and is $4 if purchased on or before March 1 or $5 if purchased at the gate. Children 5 years old and under are admitted free with a paying adult. However, children 3 years old and older will be required to have a reserved seat for concerts. Reserved seat tickets for concerts are $10 to $25. Limited free-seating is also available for most shows with your gate admission on a first come, first served basis.
Contact Information:	(813) 752-9194, berryinfo@flstrawberryfestival.com, http://www.flstrawberryfestival.com
Description:	Ranking among the top food festivals in North America, this festival dates back to 1930 and is a celebration of the strawberry harvest. It offers a variety of activities for young and old. Numerous exhibits featuring agriculture, commerce, industry, livestock, fine arts, horticulture, homemade goods, and crafts are on display daily. A wide assortment of contests (the strawberry shortcake eating my personal favorite) bring out the competitive spirit of both youth and adults. Other attractions

include a large midway with carnival games and rides, parades complete with floats and marching bands, and headliner country music entertainers who perform twice daily (there is limited free seating or reserved seats can be purchased for an additional fee). An annual scholarship pageant for the selection and coronation of the Florida Strawberry Festival® Queen highlights this festival. Of course, the main attraction is the strawberries—strawberry shortcake, strawberry milkshakes, strawberry sundaes, strawberry cobbler, strawberry ice cream, and just plain strawberries! Strawberries are also available for purchase.

FLORAL CITY STRAWBERRY FESTIVAL ~ *Great for Kids!*

City/County/Region: Floral City / Citrus / Central West
Location: Floral Park located on Hwy. 41, 2 ½ miles south of Floral City
General Date: 1st weekend in March
Duration: 2 days
Year Started: 1988
Approx. Attendance: 27,000
Public Admission Fee: $
Other Fees/Costs: Admission is $2 per person, children under 12 years old are admitted free.
Contact Information: (352) 726-2801, ccommerce1@tampabay.rr.com, http://www.citruscountychamber.com/strawberryfest.htm
Description: Strawberrries galore and and other delicious food. Art, crafts, games, contest, prizes, live entertainment, antique car show, pageant, children's activities.

THE BIG SQUEEZE ~ *Great for Kids!*

City/County/Region:	Palm Bay / Brevard / Central East
Location:	Fair Grounds at Brevard Community College-Palm Bay Campus on San Filippo Drive SE
General Date:	1st weekend in April
Duration:	4 days
Year Started:	2000
Approx. Attendance:	25,000
Public Admission Fee:	Free
Other Fees/Costs:	Unavailable
Contact Information:	(321) 951-9998, dawn@palmbaychamber.com, http://www.bigsqueezefestival.com
Description:	Statewide juice festival promoting citrus, exotic fruit and vegetable juices and related products produced in Florida. Free tastings (fruits and juice), live music entertainment, cooking shows, arts and crafts, cookoff, farmers market, carnival.

BRADFORD COUNTY STRAWBERRY FESTIVAL ~ *Great for Kids!*

City/County/Region:	Starke / Bradford / North Central
Location:	Historic Downtown Call Street
General Date:	4th weekend in April
Duration:	2 days
Year Started:	1999
Approx. Attendance:	8,000
Public Admission Fee:	Free
Other Fees/Costs:	Unavailable
Contact Information:	(904) 964-5278, specialevents@atlantic.net, http://www.northfloridachamber.com
Description:	Arts and crafts, food, live entertainment, car show, children's fun area. And, of course, lots of strawberries!

Arcadia Watermelon Festival ~ *Great for Kids!*

City/County/Region: Arcadia / Desoto / Central West
Location: Historic Downtown
General Date: 1st Saturday in May
Duration: 1 day
Year Started: Unavailable
Approx. Attendance: Varies
Public Admission Fee: Unknown
Other Fees/Costs: Unavailable
Contact Information: (863) 494-2020, peddler@strato.net
Description: Day of beauty queens (Sugar Babe, Crimson Sweet, Arcadia Watermelon Princess, Miss Jubilee and Arcadia Watermelon Queen), seed-spitting contests, music, car shows, kids games, and a whole lot of fun. And, of course, lots of watermelon! Final festivity is the Watermelon Auction where everyone is welcome to bid on wonderful watermelon goodies for the home, yard and body.

DeSoto County Watermelon Festival

City/County/Region: Arcadia / Desoto / Central West
Location: Arcadia
General Date: 1st Saturday in May
Duration: 1 day
Year Started: Unavailable
Approx. Attendance: Varies
Public Admission Fee: Unknown
Other Fees/Costs: Unavailable
Contact Information: (863) 494-4033, DawnBallard@DeSotoChamber.net, http://www.desotochamber.net, Alternative contact: DeSoto

County Historical Society, Inc. http://www.historicdesoto.org/Events.html, (863)244-9638

Description: Plenty of watermelon, beauty pageant, golf scramble, antique autos on display, and horse show.

NEWBERRY WATERMELON FESTIVAL ~ *Great for Kids!*

City/County/Region: Newberry / Alachua / North Central
Location: Canterbury Equestrian Showplace, 23100 W. Newberry Road
General Date: 2nd weekend in May
Duration: 3 days
Year Started: 1946
Approx. Attendance: Varies
Public Admission Fee: Free
Other Fees/Costs: $1 admission to pageants.
Contact Information: (352) 316-6628, newberrywatermelonfestival@yahoo.com, http://www.newberrywatermelonfestival.com
Description: Free watermelon slices. Carnival, pageants, parade, rides, 5K run. Contests include: Hog Calling, Watermelon Roll (limited to 5 year olds and under), Seed Spitting, Watermelon Eating, Pie/Cake Baking. Additional events held on Thursday and Friday. Sponsored by Florida Rock Industries.

CHIEFLAND WATERMELON FESTIVAL ~ *Great for Kids!*

City/County/Region: Chiefland / Levy / North Central
Location: Main Street and Park Avenue in downtown Chiefland

4 - Fruit Medley

General Date: 1st Saturday in June
Duration: 1 day
Year Started: 1954
Approx. Attendance: 2,000
Public Admission Fee: Free
Other Fees/Costs: Unavailable
Contact Information: (352) 493-1849, info@chieflandchamber.com, http://www.chieflandchamber.com/watermelon_fest.html
Description: Enjoy watermelon donated by local farmers. Plenty of children's activities, including a watermelon seed-spitting contest! The watermelon parade, auction, weighing-contest, and the Watermelon Queen contest are just some of the festival highlights. Arts and crafts exhibits from around Florida and neighboring states. Sponsored by the Chiefland Womens' club.

WELLBORN BLUEBERRY FESTIVAL

City/County/Region: Wellborn / Suwannee / North Central
Location: Middle of town
General Date: 1st Saturday in June
Duration: 1 day
Year Started: 2005
Approx. Attendance: 8,000
Public Admission Fee: Free
Other Fees/Costs: Parking is free.
Contact Information: (386) 208-1733, Alternative contact: (386) 963-3412
Description: Celebrates the blueberry harvest with arts, crafts, entertainment, and food. The festival has approximately 40-50 craft vendors, a variety of

food vendors, a blueberry pancake breakfast and parade in the morning, blueberries for sale, and a variety of other family activities. Hosted by the Wellborn Community Association.

JEFFERSON COUNTY WATERMELON FESTIVAL – *Great for Kids!*

City/County/Region:	Monticello / Jefferson / North Central
Location:	Downtown Monticello
General Date:	3rd weekend in June
Duration:	2 days
Year Started:	1949
Approx. Attendance:	10,000
Public Admission Fee:	Free
Other Fees/Costs:	Unavailable
Contact Information:	(850) 997-5552, info@monticellojeffersonfl.com, http://www.monticellojeffersonfl.com/festival.html
Description:	Includes beauty pageants, dinners, street dance, barn dance, arts and crafts, melon run, sports events (e.g., softball tournament), fashion show, rodeo, and parade. Some events held during the preceding weeks starting June 1 so check the website for activity schedule.

NORTHEAST FLORIDA BLUEBERRIES & BARBECUE FESTIVAL

City/County/Region:	Callahan / Nassau / Northeast
Location:	Northeast Florida Fairgrounds, 1.2 miles north of Callahan, FL on U.S. Highway #1
General Date:	2nd or 3rd weekend in June
Duration:	2 days
Year Started:	2004
Approx. Attendance:	Varies

4 - Fruit Medley

Public Admission Fee: Unknown
Other Fees/Costs: Contest entry fees are $65 for each category (chicken, ribs, pork, brisket, People's Choice), $25 for "Anything But" contest, $10 for blueberry recipe cookoff.
Contact Information: (904) 879-1359, jarrett_d@neflfair.org, http://www.neflfair.org, Alternative contact: (904) 879-4682, http://www.greaternassaucounty.com, (904) 879-1441
Description: Blueberry pancake breakfast. On Saturday only, barbecue cook-off contest with categories for chicken, ribs, pork, brisket, and overall. Street dance. Sponsored by the Northeast Florida Fair Association. See listing on http://www.flbbq.org for more information regarding the barbecue competition.

BOSTWICK BLUEBERRY FESTIVAL - *Great for Kids!*

City/County/Region: Bostwick / Putnam / Northeast
Location: Bostwick Community Center, 125 Tillman St.
General Date: 3rd weekend in June
Duration: 1 day
Year Started: 1996
Approx. Attendance: 8,000
Public Admission Fee: Free
Other Fees/Costs: Unavailable
Contact Information: (386) 328-2497, everton189@aol.com, http://mybcai.tripod.com/id6.html
Description: Enjoy a pancake breakfast, more than 10,000 pounds of blueberries, and homemade baked goods. Activities include a blueberry cookoff, monster truck show, entertainment, clown, magician, children's games, arts and crafts and

93

a petting zoo. There is a blueberry bake-off held the night before the festival. Also, the Bostwick Cookbook, featuring local southern cuisine (not just blueberries), will be available. 2006 will be the 10th anniversary so there may be some special, additional activities.

PANHANDLE WATERMELON FESTIVAL ~ *Great for Kids!*

City/County/Region: Chipley / Washington / Northwest
Location: Agricultural Center on Jackson Ave., Hwy 90
General Date: 4th full weekend in June
Duration: 2 days
Year Started: Unavailable
Approx. Attendance: Varies
Public Admission Fee: Free
Other Fees/Costs: Unavailable
Contact Information: (850) 638-6180, washington@ifas.ufl.edu, http://www.thewtdc.com/home/events/watermellonfestival, Alternative contact: Washington County Chamber, wcchamber@wfeca.net, (850) 638-4157, http://www.washcomall.com
Description: Festival events include a watermelon contest, concerts, square dancing, arts and crafts, antique car show, children's games, and much more! Every year the big Watermelon Parade is held before the kick-off of festival activities.

INTERNATIONAL MANGO FESTIVAL ~ *Great for Kids!*

City/County/Region: Coral Gables / Miami-Dade / Southeast
Location: Fairchild Tropical Botanic Garden, 10901 Old Cutler Road

General Date:	2nd weekend in July
Duration:	2 days
Year Started:	1993
Approx. Attendance:	Varies
Public Admission Fee:	$$
Other Fees/Costs:	Must pay admission to the Fairchild Tropical Botanic Garden. Admission is $20 for adults, $15 Senior citizens 65 and older, $10 for children 6 - 17, and free for Fairchild members and children 5 and under.
Contact Information:	(305) 667-1651, pfernandez@fairchildgarden.org, http://www.fairchildgarden.org/horticulture/mangofest.html
Description:	Taste the many flavors of the mango, buy a mango tree perfect for your own garden, learn how to grow healthy trees that produce luscious fruit, enjoy children's activities, participate in the Mango Cook-off, try mango cuisine at the Mango Brunch and participate in the live Mango Auction.

FLORIDA KEYS TROPICAL FRUIT FIESTA ~ *Great for Kids!*

City/County/Region:	Key West / Monroe / Southwest
Location:	Florida Keys (rotates between Key West, Key Largo, and Marathon)
General Date:	Saturday in mid-July
Duration:	1 day
Year Started:	1998
Approx. Attendance:	2,500
Public Admission Fee:	Free
Other Fees/Costs:	Unavailable
Contact Information:	(305) 292-4501, monroe@ifas.ufl.edu, http://monroe.ifas.ufl.edu/fruitfiesta.htm, Alternative

Food Fest! Your Complete Guide to Florida's Food Festivals

contact: lindley-cristina@monroecounty-fl.gov

Description: Buy healthy fruit trees, eat delicious tropical fruit and tropical fruit ice cream. Attend tropical fruit lectures given by University of Florida Tropical fruit experts. Enter the Home Grown Fruit Contest. Plant clinic and auction, food, games for kids, vendors, and entertainment.

MANGOMANIA TROPICAL FRUIT FAIR ~ *Great for Kids!*

City/County/Region: Pine Island / Lee / Southwest
Location: German American Club, Pine Island Road (S.R. 78)
General Date: 3rd weekend in July
Duration: 2 days
Year Started: 1997
Approx. Attendance: 10,000
Public Admission Fee: $
Other Fees/Costs: Adult admission $6, children under 10 are free. Includes free parking.
Contact Information: (239) 283-0888, Info@pineislandchamber.org, http://www.mangomaniafl.com
Description: Mango and tropical fruit specialties and tasting, live musical entertainment, arts and crafts, lots of unique contests, children's activities.

JENSEN BEACH PINEAPPLE FESTIVAL ~ *Great for Kids!*

City/County/Region: Jensen Beach / Martin / Southeast
Location: Historic downtown
General Date: 1st weekend in November
Duration: 3 days

Year Started:	1988
Approx. Attendance:	30,000
Public Admission Fee:	$
Other Fees/Costs:	Admission fees are $5 on Friday from 6pm-midnight, $5 on Saturday from 11am-midnight, $10 on Saturday after 6pm, 2 for $5 on Sunday from 1pm-midnight.
Contact Information:	(772) 334-7755, jb-mainstreet@aol.com, http://www.jensenbeachmainstreet.com, Alternative contact: http://www.jensenbeachfestivals.com
Description:	Chocolate-covered pineapples! Activities for kids of all ages including national and regional musical entertainment, local bands, amusement rides, food court, arts and crafts village, street entertainment (e.g., strolling barbershop quartets, solo guitar artists, mimes, clowns), children's activity area, and many more unique attractions. Sponsored by Jensen Beach Mainstreet.

5   Vegan's Variety

For health-conscious festival-goers, there's a cornucopia of festivals celebrating vegetables. The Swamp Cabbage festival honors the delicacy gourmets call the "Heart of Palm," the meat of the cabbage palm tree. The cabbage palm is actually the Sabal Palm, which is the official state tree of Florida. Like most vegetables, swamp cabbage is low in saturated fat and very low in cholesterol. If that's too daring, there are plenty of other vegetables—Florida growers harvest enough veggies to rank Florida among the top five states nationally in overall vegetable cash receipts. Additionally, Florida leads the nation in cash receipts for tomatoes and sugarcane. Have a healthy heart and pay tribute to the state's hardworking farmers by attending a veggie fest!

So many pumpkins, so little time!

DELRAY BEACH GARLIC FEST ~ *Great for Kids!*

City/County/Region: Delray Beach / Palm Beach / Southeast
Location: Downtown, Between the Historical Old School Square Grounds and NE 2nd Ave.
General Date: 3rd weekend in February
Duration: 3 days
Year Started: 1999
Approx. Attendance: 30,000
Public Admission Fee: $
Other Fees/Costs: Admission fee is $8 ($1 of every ticket purchased goes to Project Thanksgiving).
Contact Information: (561) 279-0907, nancy@avenuecreative.com, http://www.dbgarlicfest.com
Description: A gourmet food and entertainment event that features unique and original garlic-laced dishes, including garlic ice cream! Garlic-themed memorabilia. Attend Garlic University where you can learn everything you ever wanted to know about garlic but were afraid to ask. Viking's Garlic Chef Stadium features the world's own Garlic Chef Competition. Cloves and Vines Wine Garden features fine wines from around the world. Live national act entertainment, children's area.

SWAMP CABBAGE FESTIVAL ~ *Great for Kids!*

City/County/Region: La Belle / Hendry / Southwest
Location: Barron Park, along the banks of the Caloosahatchee River
General Date: Last weekend in February
Duration: 3 days
Year Started: 1965
Approx. Attendance: 25,000

Public Admission Fee:	Free
Other Fees/Costs:	Tickets for rodeo are $12 for adults, $6 for kids age 7-17, kids 6 and under are free.
Contact Information:	(863) 675-2995, chair@swampcabbagefestival.com, http://www.swampcabbagefestival.com
Description:	This festival honors the delicacy gourmets call the Heart of Palm, the meat of the cabbage palm tree. The cabbage palm is actually the Sabal Palm, which is the state tree of Florida. The festival also features a parade, rodeo, arts and crafts, Indian food and crafts, live entertainment, and cornonation of the Miss Swamp Cabbage Queen.

Sugar Festival ~ *Great for Kids!*

City/County/Region:	Clewiston / Hendry / Southwest
Location:	Civic City Park and the surrounding areas
General Date:	3rd or 4th Saturday in April
Duration:	1 day
Year Started:	1985
Approx. Attendance:	20,000
Public Admission Fee:	Free
Other Fees/Costs:	Unavailable
Contact Information:	(863) 983-7979, clewistonchamber@earthlink.net, http://www.clewiston.org/festival.htm
Description:	Festival attractions include an arts and crafts show, a car show, exhibits of old and new farming equipment, and an old-fashioned cane grinding. Booths featuring local and regional food will serve all day. There's also a horseshoe tournament, rodeo, a bass tournament, and an art show and quilt exhibition. A Fun Park featuring a rock-climbing wall and a giant slide

and carousel. One of the most popular events is the Sweet Taste of Sugar Country Dessert Contest.

SWEET CORN FIESTA ~ *Great for Kids!*

City/County/Region: West Palm Beach / Palm Beach / Southeast
Location: Yesteryear Village on South Florida Fairgrounds
General Date: Last Sunday in April
Duration: 1 day
Year Started: 2001
Approx. Attendance: 6,000
Public Admission Fee: $
Other Fees/Costs: Admission is $5 for adults, $3 for children 6-11, kids 5 and under free.
Contact Information: (561) 793-0333, jennifer@southfloridafair.com, http://www.southfloridafair.com
Description: Mouth-watering and locally grown sweet corn. Children rides, games and activities, live musical entertainment, Sweet Corn Shuckin' Contest, National Corn Eating Contest, local Corn Eating Contest, Old-fashioned Bathing Suit competition.

RUSKIN TOMATO FESTIVAL ~ *Great for Kids!*

City/County/Region: Ruskin / Hillsborough / Central West
Location: E. G. Simmons County Park
General Date: 1st weekend in May
Duration: 2 days
Year Started: 1997
Approx. Attendance: 7,000

Public Admission Fee: $

Other Fees/Costs: $4 admission, children under 6 are free,

Contact Information: (813) 363-5438, postmaster@ruskinfoundation.org, http://ruskinfoundation.org/festival.html, Alternative contact: (813) 645-3808

Description: Free tomato plants to first 250 people, free sliced tomatoes, fried green tomatoes, Tomato Queen pageant, antique car and tractor show, live music entertainment, kid's activities, arts and crafts.

WINDSOR ZUCCHINI FESTIVAL ~ *Great for Kids!*

City/County/Region: Gainesville / Alachua / North Central

Location: Windsor Volunteer Fire Station, 1401 SE CR 234

General Date: 2nd Saturday in May

Duration: 1 day

Year Started: 1981

Approx. Attendance: Varies

Public Admission Fee: Unknown

Other Fees/Costs: Unavailable

Contact Information: (352) 378-8671, windsor@afn.org, http://www.afn.org/~windsor/page2.html

Description: Fried zucchini, zucchini ice cream, zucchini cooking contest, zucchini carving contest. Duke of Zuke & Zuqueenie Pageant, Zucchinithon fun run, music, rides, kid's activities, arts and crafts. Benefiting the Windsor Volunteer Fire Department.

Zellwood Sweet Corn Festival ~ *Great for Kids!*

City/County/Region: Zellwood / Orange / Central
Location: Festival Grounds located at 4253 W Ponkan Rd
General Date: Last weekend in May
Duration: 2 days
Year Started: 1971
Approx. Attendance: 19,000
Public Admission Fee: $$
Other Fees/Costs: Tickets for adults are $20 in advance or $25 the day of the show. Children 12 and under get in free with paid adult. Prices include parking, arts and crafts show, entertainment, corn eating contest, and all the Zellwood Corn you can Eat! Advance ride band can be purchased from the festival office in advance for $12 or $15 day of event.
Contact Information: (407) 886-0014, zellcorn@earthlink.net, http://www.zellwoodcornfestival.com
Description: Corn eating and corn shucking contests, fresh corn for sale, arts and crafts, live music entertainment, amusement rides. Watch "BIG BERTHA" at work—she can cook 1,650 ears of corn every 9 minutes, in 350 gallons of boiling water!

Central Florida Peanut Festival ~ *Great for Kids!*

City/County/Region: Williston / Levy / North Central
Location: Linear Park, N. Main St.
General Date: 1st Saturday in October
Duration: 1 day
Year Started: 1988
Approx. Attendance: 5,000

Public Admission Fee: Free
Other Fees/Costs: Unavailable
Contact Information: (352) 528-5552, wcoc@willistonfl.com, http://www.willistonfl.com
Description: All things peanut! Raw peanuts, peanut treats, peanut novalties as well as a variety of food, juried arts and crafts area, and other vendors. Entertainment all day. Little Peanut Queen, King and Baby contest. Rides for the children.

GABBERT FARM PEANUT FESTIVAL ~ *Great for Kids!*

City/County/Region: Jay / Santa Rosa / Northwest
Location: Gabbert Farm, 3604 Pine Level Church Road, 4 1/2 miles south off Hwy 89
General Date: 1st full weekend in October
Duration: 2 days
Year Started: 1990
Approx. Attendance: 50,000
Public Admission Fee: Free
Other Fees/Costs: Free parking.
Contact Information: (850) 675-6823
Description: Featuring peanuts—green, boiled, roasted, fried and candied. Activities include pony rides, hay rides, moon walk, rock climbing, anvil shoot, and pedal tractor pull. Large display of fully restored tractor and antique farm equipment, 1930s farm museum, antique shop, and gristmill. Competitions include bubble gum contest, pig chase, and pet dress-up parade and contest. Music and many more activities. Wide variety of foods such as barbecue, fish and chicken dinners, carnival fare, and baked goods.

Hunsader Farms Pumpkin Festival ~ *Great for Kids!*

City/County/Region: Bradenton / Manatee / Central West
Location: Hunsader Farms, 5100 County Road 675 (between State Road 64 and State Road 70)
General Date: Last 3 weekends in October
Duration: 5 days
Year Started: 1992
Approx. Attendance: Varies
Public Admission Fee: $
Other Fees/Costs: Admission is $6, parking fee $2. Children 12 and under free. Concert day admission $8.
Contact Information: (941) 322-2168, dkhunsader@msn.com, http://www.hunsaderfarms.com
Description: Lots of food—fresh roasted sweet corn, BBQ, pumpkin pie, apple cider, and much more! Craft booths, country music, clogging, chainsaw sculpting, circus tent, fresh produce, and kid's activities including hay and pony rides, petting zoo, barnyard playground.

6   Drink, Drank, Drunk

From one who's known (at least in my family) for coining the time "beer-thirty," this is my favorite chapter! A trip to Europe transformed me into somewhat of a beer snob, so I challenge you to come out of your beer stein and taste test some unique and different brews. Drink outside the beer bottle—and definitely outside the wine box! But whichever you choose, please drink responsibly. A fair warning for those who prefer wine—most events charge admission fees, so make sure you ask ahead of time. Cheers!

I can name this wine with my eyes closed!

NAPLES WINTER WINE FESTIVAL

City/County/Region: Naples / Collier / Southwest
Location: Ritz-Carlton Golf Resort
General Date: Last weekend in January
Duration: 3 days
Year Started: 2001
Approx. Attendance: 550
Public Admission Fee: $$$
Other Fees/Costs: $7,500 for two people to attend all the events and be driven by private car to the vintner dinner.
Contact Information: (239) 514-2239, info@napleswinefestival.com, http://www.napleswinefestival.com, Alternative contact: (888) 837-4919
Description: Charity wine event featuring a vintner dinner, live auction, and Sunday brunch. The vintner dinners include celebrity chefs like Emeril Lagasse cooking for small groups and a chance to uncork prized wines seated next to the vintner who made them. Proceeds from the wine auction benefit local area children's charities.

EINSTEIN ON WINE

City/County/Region: Tampa / Hillsborough / Central West
Location: Museum of Science and Industry
General Date: 1st Saturday in February
Duration: 1 day
Year Started: 1996
Approx. Attendance: Varies
Public Admission Fee: $$$
Other Fees/Costs: Tickets are $50 for MOSI members, $60 for nonmembers, and $70 at the door.

Contact Information: (813) 987-6100, cstreet@mosi.org, http://www.mosi.org/specialevents.html

Description: Hosted by BEAM (Be Enthusiastic About MOSI) and ABC Fine Wine & Spirits, "Einstein on Wine" combines wine, food, music, and a silent auction in a fundraising event for all to enjoy. More than 80 vintners offer tastings on all varieties of wines—reds, whites, champagnes, domestic and imported. All proceeds benefit MOSI's education programs.

LAKERIDGE WINEFEST

City/County/Region: Clermont / Lake / Central
Location: Lakeridge Winery, 19239 U.S. 27 North
General Date: Last weekend in February
Duration: 3 days
Year Started: 1992
Approx. Attendance: Varies
Public Admission Fee: $
Other Fees/Costs: Admission is $2 and supports the South Lake Chamber of Commerce.
Contact Information: (800) 768-9463, http://www.lakeridgewinery.com/aboutus-events.php3, Alternative contact: http://www.southlakechamber-fl.com, (352) 394-4191, maryj@southlakechamber-fl.com
Description: Free winery walking tours and tastings, live music on outdoor stage, arts and crafts, food and wine for purchase. Parking is free and there's ample seating, but can bring blankets and chairs. Event is co-hosted by Lakeridge and the South Lake Chamber of Commerce.

SOUTH BEACH WINE AND FOOD FESTIVAL

City/County/Region: Miami / Miami-Dade / Southeast
Location: South Beach
General Date: Last weekend in February
Duration: 3 days
Year Started: 2002
Approx. Attendance: 23,000
Public Admission Fee: $$$
Other Fees/Costs: Ticket prices vary, $75 and up, depending on event.
Contact Information: (305) 627-1134, Lori-AnnCox@SOUTHERNWINE.com, http://www.sobewineandfoodfest.com
Description: Event showcases the talents of the world's most renowned wine and spirits producers, chefs and culinary personalities. Culinary demonstrations, wine seminars, wine and spirit tastings, food tastings, gourmet dinners, food and wine pairings and much more. Upscale festival for epicureans. Hosted by Southern Wine & Spirits of Florida and Florida International University (FIU), the festival benefits the Teaching Restaurant and the Southern Wine & Spirits Beverage Management Center both located at FIU. No one under 21 permitted in the Grand Tasting Village.

SAN SEBASTIAN WINEFEST

City/County/Region: St. Augustine / St. Johns / Northeast
Location: San Sebastian Winery, 157 King Street
General Date: Last weekend in February
Duration: 2 days

Year Started:	2003
Approx. Attendance:	Varies
Public Admission Fee:	Free
Other Fees/Costs:	Unavailable
Contact Information:	(904) 826-1594, eleyda@sansebastianwinery.com, http://www.sansebastianwinery.com/events.html, Alternative contact: (888) 352-9463
Description:	Celebrate new wine releases at San Sebastian Winery. Complimentary tours and wine tasting offered all weekend. Local artists display and sell their original work. Cooking demonstrations by students of the Southeast Institute of Culinary Arts. Live music in 'The Cellar Upstairs' Wine and Jazz Bar during the entire weekend on the open-air deck. Selection of San Sebastian wine, imported beers, soft drinks and light appetizers available for purchase.

FLORIDA BREWERS GUILD BEERFEST

City/County/Region:	Tampa / Hillsborough / Central West
Location:	Centro Ybor City
General Date:	1st Saturday in March
Duration:	1 day
Year Started:	1997
Approx. Attendance:	1,500
Public Admission Fee:	$$
Other Fees/Costs:	Tickets $20 in advance, $25 day of show.
Contact Information:	(727) 866-7350, fbguild@aol.com, http://www.floridabrewersguild.org
Description:	Sample over 100 of Florida's best craft beers. Live music. Everyone receives a Florida Brewers Guild glass. Major fundraising event for the Florida Brewers Guild.

BOCA BACCHANAL WINEFEST

City/County/Region: Boca Raton / Palm Beach / Southeast
Location: Various locations including the Boca Raton Resort & Club and Centre for the Arts at Mizner Park
General Date: 2nd Friday and Saturday in March
Duration: 2 days
Year Started: Unavailable
Approx. Attendance: Varies
Public Admission Fee: $$$
Other Fees/Costs: Seminars are $10 per person, first come, first serve, but must reserve and pay online to attend. Other tickets range from $60-$300 depending on event.
Contact Information: (561) 395-6766, info@bocahistory.org, http://www.bocabacchanal.com
Description: Winefest and auction to benefit the Heritage Education programs of the Boca Raton Historical Society. Wine tastings and vintner dinners.

MIAMI WINE AND FOOD FESTIVAL

City/County/Region: Miami / Miami-Dade / Southeast
Location: InterContinental Miami, 100 Chopin Plaza
General Date: Late part of the first quarter (March or April)
Duration: 3 days
Year Started: 1996
Approx. Attendance: 1,000
Public Admission Fee: $$$
Other Fees/Costs: Tickets are $100-$500 depending on event.

Contact Information: (786) 596-9463, info@miamiwinefestival.org, http://www.miamiwineandfoodfestival.org

Description: Three-day wine and food affair features an array of culinary and wine events including wine tastings, black-tie dinners, an interactive cooking session, and live and silent auctions. Also features a golf tournament. Each event has its own fee. Ranked as one of the nation's top charity wine events, benefits United Way of Miami-Dade and Baptist Health South Florida Foundation.

FLORIDA WINE FESTIVAL

City/County/Region: Tallahassee / Leon / North Central
Location: Tallahassee
General Date: 1st Thursday through Saturday in April
Duration: 3 days
Year Started: Unavailable
Approx. Attendance: Varies
Public Admission Fee: $$$
Other Fees/Costs: Tickets $10 for tasting event, other events range from $50-$150 depending on event.
Contact Information: (850) 513-0700, info@thefloridawinefestival.com, http://www.thefloridawinefestival.com
Description: Traditional wine tasting and dinner reception. Attendees enjoy a wonderful assortment of food from event restaurants. Wine is complimentary throughout the evening. Silent and live auction. Live music. Fundraising event for The Mary Brogan Museum of Art and Science

Coral Gables Wine & Food Festival

City/County/Region: Coral Gables / Miami-Dade / Southeast
Location: Giralda Avenue (between Ponce De Leon Blvd. & Galiano Street)
General Date: 1st Thursday in April
Duration: 1 day
Year Started: 2004
Approx. Attendance: Varies
Public Admission Fee: $$$
Other Fees/Costs: Tickets for the street festival are $40, Tickets for VIP reception are $100 and include admission to the street festival.
Contact Information: (954) 524-4657, info@sflung.org, http://www.sflung.org
Description: Street festival featuring food from Coral Gables' famed "restaurant row," fine wines, and live entertainment. There is a VIP reception held prior to the street festival. Proceeds benefit the American Lung Association.

New Times Beerfest

City/County/Region: Fort Lauderdale / Broward / Southeast
Location: Downtown Fort Lauderdale on SW 2nd Street / Himmarshee at Esplanade Park
General Date: 2nd or 3rd Saturday in April
Duration: 1 day
Year Started: 1997
Approx. Attendance: 4,000
Public Admission Fee: $$
Other Fees/Costs: Tickets are $15 in advance, $20 day of Beerfest. You must be 21 or older with valid ID to attend. Tickets are non refundable rain or shine.

6 - Drink, Drank, Drunk

Contact Information: (954) 233-1559, inga.baekkelund@newtimesbpb.com, http://www.browardpalmbeach.com

Description: Join New Times Broward-Palm Beach and celebrate the best South Florida has to offer: great beer, great food, and great music at their annual Beerfest. Event features over 100 beers from around the world and delectable delights from Broward/Palm Beach area restaurants. In addition to the suds, the event showcases sounds from South Florida with live performances by some of the area's most popular local bands. You must be 21 or older with valid ID to attend. New Times introduced the original Beerfest in 1997 at the War Memorial Auditorium in Ft. Lauderdale, drawing a crowd of roughly 1,000. Due to the success of the event, Beerfest quickly outgrew this venue and moved to their bigger home in downtown Fort Lauderdale. Each year attendance and the number of beers has grown significantly.

SANDESTIN WINE FESTIVAL

City/County/Region: Sandestin / Okaloosa / Northwest
Location: The Village of Baytowne Wharf
General Date: Begins 3rd Saturday in April
Duration: 4 days
Year Started: 1986
Approx. Attendance: Varies
Public Admission Fee: $$$
Other Fees/Costs: Tickets range from $15 to $250 depending on event.

115

Contact Information: (850) 267-8092, winefestival@sandestin.com, http://www.sandestinwinefest.com

Description: Opportunity to taste and purchase more than 500 wines. Wine dinners and tastings, charity wine auction, champagne brunch.

FLORIDA WINEFEST & AUCTION

City/County/Region: Sarasota / Sarasota / Central West
Location: Ritz Carlton, St. Armands Circle
General Date: Begins 4th Thursday in April
Duration: 4 days
Year Started: 1991
Approx. Attendance: 5,000
Public Admission Fee: $$$
Other Fees/Costs: Ticket prices $40-$250 depending on event.
Contact Information: (800) 216-6199, info@floridawinefest.com, http://www.floridawinefest.com, Alternative contact: 1-877-FLA-WINE
Description: Week-long food and wine extravaganza and auction benefiting many local charities. Winemaker brunch and seminars. Wine tasting. Gala Black-tie Wine Dinner Dance. Charity wine auction.

BERN'S WINEFEST

City/County/Region: Tampa / Hillsborough / Central West
Location: SideBern's and Bern's Fine Wines & Spirits property at the corner of Howard and Morrison Avenues
General Date: Last weekend in April
Duration: 4 days

Year Started:	1998
Approx. Attendance:	Varies
Public Admission Fee:	$$$
Other Fees/Costs:	Tickets range from $95-$250 depending on event.
Contact Information:	(813) 253-0358, marketing@bernssteakhouse.com, http://www.bernswinefest.com
Description:	Tastings, educational seminars, and winemaker dinners. Proceeds benefit Make-A-Wish Foundation. Guests must be 21 years of age or over, Id required.

BILTMORE INTERNATIONAL FOOD & WINE WEEKEND

City/County/Region:	Coral Gables / Miami-Dade / Southeast
Location:	Biltmore Hotel, 1200 Anastasia Avenue
General Date:	First week in May
Duration:	3 days
Year Started:	1997
Approx. Attendance:	Varies
Public Admission Fee:	$$$
Other Fees/Costs:	Tickets $75-$195 depending on event.
Contact Information:	(305) 913-3203, cheers@thecellarclub.com, http://www.biltmorefestival.com
Description:	Three-day celebration featuring more than 70 wineries pouring All Reserve, Single Vineyard, and Upper Tier wines. Showcasing more than 20 of South Florida's top culinary talents and welcoming internationally acclaimed celebrity chefs. Golf classic, wine and food tasting, celebrity chefs dinner, culinary luncheon and silent auction.

Las Olas Wine and Food Festival

City/County/Region:	Fort Lauderdale / Broward / Southeast
Location:	East Las Olas Blvd.
General Date:	2nd Thursday in May
Duration:	1 day
Year Started:	1996
Approx. Attendance:	Varies
Public Admission Fee:	$$$
Other Fees/Costs:	Street festival tickets are $60, VIP reception tickets are $120.
Contact Information:	(954) 524-4657, info@sflung.org, http://www.lasolaswineandfood.com, Alternative contact: http://www.sflung.org
Description:	Sample the best wines and gourmet foods from the area restaurants. Musical entertainment and a fashion show add to the festivities. Sponsored by the American Lung Association.

Shores Wine and Food Festival

City/County/Region:	Daytona Beach / Volusia / Central East
Location:	The Shores Resort and Spa, 2637 South Atlantic Avenue
General Date:	Last Saturday in June
Duration:	1 day
Year Started:	2001
Approx. Attendance:	Varies
Public Admission Fee:	$$$
Other Fees/Costs:	Tickets range from $40-$95 depending on event. Packages including accomodations start at $499 per couple.

Contact Information: (386) 322-7242, contactus@shoresresort.com, http://www.shoreswineandfoodfest.com, Alternative contact: The Shores Resort & Spa, http://www.shoresresort.com

Description: Celebration of wine, food, and music. Activities include a wine tasting, food and wine pairing, seminars, over 100 wines from around the world, and a silent auction benefiting The Betty Jane France Pediatrics Center Home of Speediatrics at Halifax Medical Center in Daytona Beach.

Key West Food and Wine Festival

City/County/Region: Key West / Monroe / Southwest
Location: La Concha Hotel, 430 Duval Street
General Date: Begins last Friday in July
Duration: 10 days
Year Started: Unavailable
Approx. Attendance: Varies
Public Admission Fee: $$$
Other Fees/Costs: Tickets range from $10-$85 depending on event.
Contact Information: (305) 296-6909, kwrba@aol.com, http://www.kwrba.com/festival.htm
Description: Ten days of food events including special dinners honoring specific foods or wines, wine and food pairings, cooking classes, and the popular "Battle of the Bars"—many other events too numerous to mention.

Food Fest! Your Complete Guide to Florida's Food Festivals

Folio Weekly Beer & Music Festival

City/County/Region:	Jacksonville / Duval / Northeast
Location:	Alltel Stadium, Touchdown Club West
General Date:	1st Friday in July
Duration:	1 day
Year Started:	1996
Approx. Attendance:	Varies
Public Admission Fee:	$$
Other Fees/Costs:	Tickets are $25 in advance at any of the participating ticket outlets, and $30 at the door. Ticket price includes a complimenary mug or glass.
Contact Information:	(904) 564-1894, planet@planetradio933.com, http://www.folioweeklybeerfest.com/main.html, Alternative contact: http://jaxbeerfest.com/main.html
Description:	Sample more than 100 beers and food from local restaurants. Live music from area bands. No one under 21 admitted!

Gavel & Grapes Festival

City/County/Region:	Tarpon Springs / Pinellas / Central West
Location:	Downtown on Tarpon Avenue
General Date:	In July
Duration:	1 day
Year Started:	1999
Approx. Attendance:	Varies
Public Admission Fee:	$$$
Other Fees/Costs:	$35 for unlimited wine and beer tasting, $5 admission for others, children under 12 free.
Contact Information:	(727) 741-3647, forms@tarpontsba.com, http://www.gavelandgrapes.com

6 - Drink, Drank, Drunk

Description: Evening of tasting various wines from around the world, boutique beers, food, entertainment, arts and crafts, car show, absolute auction.

[handwritten: Hensvratch Farms Annual Grape Stomp & Music Fest - August (see back) (over)]

WaZoo

City/County/Region: Tampa / Hillsborough / Central West
Location: Tampa's Lowry Park Zoo
General Date: 1st Saturday in August
Duration: 1 day
Year Started: 1996
Approx. Attendance: 4,000
Public Admission Fee: $$
Other Fees/Costs: Tickets prices vary depending upon type. For example, one includes both food and beers, another is a Designated Driver ticket which includes only the food.
Contact Information: (813) 935-8552, information@lowryparkzoo.com, http://www.lowryparkzoo.com
Description: This tropical taste explosion features beverage samplings from breweries worldwide and a beautiful wine garden. Several restaurants provide a tantalizing selection of local cuisine, and guests can dance or relax with a variety of live entertainment throughout the evening. All proceeds from the event benefit the animals and education programs at the Zoo.

San Sebastian Harvest Festival & Grape Stomp

City/County/Region: St. Augustine / St. Johns / Northeast
Location: San Sebastian Winery at 157 King Street
General Date: Last weekend in August
Duration: 2 days

121

Year Started:	1998
Approx. Attendance:	Varies
Public Admission Fee:	Free
Other Fees/Costs:	Admission is free and there is plenty of parking available. An optional $2 donation benefiting the First Coast Institute's School of Culinary Arts, Local Scholarship Program will be accepted.
Contact Information:	(904) 826-1594, eleyda@sansebastianwinery.com, http://www.sansebastianwinery.com/events.html
Description:	Celebrates Harvest of the Grapes. Grape stomping competitions run throughout the entire weekend with prizes awarded to the winners. Complimentary tours and wine tasting offered. Live music.

EMERALD COAST BREW FEST & BEACH PARTY

City/County/Region:	Pensacola / Escambia / Northwest
Location:	Seville Quarter, 130 E Government St.
General Date:	The weekend after Labor Day
Duration:	2 days
Year Started:	1995
Approx. Attendance:	750
Public Admission Fee:	$$
Other Fees/Costs:	Tickets are $15 in advance, $20 at door. Admission to Beach Party is $10.
Contact Information:	(850) 221-8153, payme2@cox.net, http://www.emeraldcoastbeerfest.com
Description:	Friday night features over 200 fine crafted beers, wines and ciders from breweries, homebrew clubs, and distributors. Beers from around the world. Saturday features a Beach Party and Beer

Olympics where teams compete for the 'Horn of Thor.' Also entertainment from live bands.

Epcot Food and Wine Festival

City/County/Region: Orlando / Orange / Central
Location: Epcot at Walt Disney World, Interstate 4, Exit 64
General Date: Begins in October and runs 6 weeks
Duration: 45 days
Year Started: 1996
Approx. Attendance: Varies
Public Admission Fee: $$$
Other Fees/Costs: Epcot admission required. Some seminars free, food tastes nominal charge.
Contact Information: (407) 939-3378, http://www.disneyworld.com/foodandwine, Alternative contact: (407) 824-4321
Description: Food and wine from around the world and food tastes from various regions. More than 100 wineries and breweries present samplings, seminars, and culinary demonstrations. Concert each evening, 10K Run.

Fine Wine & Food Festival

City/County/Region: Oldsmar / Pinellas / Central West
Location: Nielsen Grand Hall and Lakeside Garden at Media Research on Brooker Creek Parkway
General Date: 2nd Friday in November
Duration: 1 day
Year Started: Unavailable
Approx. Attendance: Varies

Public Admission Fee: $$
Other Fees/Costs: Tickets are $25 in advance and $30 day of show.
Contact Information: (813) 884-5344, dpaul@UTBchamber.com, http://www.oldsmarchamber.org
Description: Features an outstanding wine list from across the country and around the world, great food to please the palate courtesy of many fine dining establishments in the local area. Music, dancing, and live and silent auctions. Fundraiser for the Upper Tampa Bay Chamber Education Foundation.

Tallahassee Wine and Food Festival

City/County/Region: Tallahassee / Leon / North Central
Location: University Center Club at Florida State University
General Date: Begins 2nd Thursday in November
Duration: 3 days
Year Started: 1996
Approx. Attendance: 650
Public Admission Fee: $$$
Other Fees/Costs: Tickets range from $50-$225 depending on event.
Contact Information: (850) 222-0200, felina@youreventions.com, http://www.tallywinefest.org, Alternative contact: March of Dimes, (850) 422-3152
Description: Wine Tasting offering an assortment of over 200 wines from around the world, live music and hors d' oeuvres. Over 150 items are auctioned (from vintage wines to 7-day get-a-way trips). Benefits the March of Dimes.

Safety Harbor Wine Festival

City/County/Region: Safety Harbor / Pinellas / Central West
Location: Main Street, between Bayshore Blvd & 8th Ave.
General Date: 1st Saturday in November
Duration: 1 day
Year Started: 2002
Approx. Attendance: 12,500
Public Admission Fee: Free
Other Fees/Costs: Wine samples are $3, $5, and $10.
Contact Information: (727) 724-1572, jcooper@cityofsafetyharbor.com, http://www.cityofsafetyharbor.com
Description: Wine tasting, live entertainment, grape stomping, silent auction, arts and crafts. Proceeds benefit local charities and civic organizations.

Dunedin Wines the Blues

City/County/Region: Dunedin / Pinellas / Central West
Location: Main Street
General Date: 2nd Saturday in November
Duration: 1 day
Year Started: 1992
Approx. Attendance: 30,000
Public Admission Fee: $
Other Fees/Costs: $1 donation required before food and wine purchases. Must purchase wristband to drink (nominal fee).
Contact Information: (727) 733-3197, chamber@dunedin-fl.com, http://www.dunedin-fl.com, Alternative contact: http://www.delightfuldunedin.com
Description: Wine and beer samplings, crafters, and live entertainment. Food from local restaurants. Sponsored by the Downtown Merchants Assn.

ORLANDO BEER FESTIVAL

City/County/Region: Orlando / Orange / Central
Location: Universal CityWalk®
General Date: 2nd weekend in November
Duration: 2 days
Year Started: 1999
Approx. Attendance: Varies
Public Admission Fee: $$
Other Fees/Costs: Tickets for Saturday are $30.95 in advance, and $37.95 the day of. Tickets for Sunday are $22.95 in advance, and $29.95 the day of. VIP tickets, which include access to the three private food and beverage areas of the event, may be purchased as a $20 upgrade to the daily ticket.
Contact Information: (407) 224-5386, http://www.orlandobeerfestival.com
Description: Taste beers from around the world! In addition to the hundreds of beverages to be sampled, the festival features live music performances accompanied by A Taste of CityWalk, where you can enjoy the world class CityWalk restaurants' flavorful and diverse tastes. The Taste of CityWalk food samples are not included in the price of the event ticket.

7   Miscellaneous Munchies

Simply because some festivals don't fall nice and neat into one of the previous categories doesn't mean they should be overlooked (especially the pie festival). Who among you hasn't wanted to skip the entrée on occasion and go straight to dessert? I don't have to tell you how I feel about the chocolate festival—yum, yum!

Enjoying a decadent dessert at a chocolate festival.

Honey Festival

City/County/Region:	La Belle / Glades / Southwest
Location:	Muse Fire Department
General Date:	2nd Saturday in January
Duration:	1 day
Year Started:	Unavailable
Approx. Attendance:	Varies
Public Admission Fee:	Unknown
Other Fees/Costs:	Unavailable
Contact Information:	(863) 946-0440, gccommerce@gladesonline.com, http://www.gladesonline.com, Alternative contact: Muse Community Center, (863) 674-0773
Description:	Honey, honey, and more honey!

Taste of Chocolate Festival

City/County/Region:	Plant City / Hillsborough / Central West
Location:	McCall Park, 100 N Collins St.
General Date:	2nd Saturday in February
Duration:	1 day
Year Started:	Unavailable
Approx. Attendance:	Varies
Public Admission Fee:	Free
Other Fees/Costs:	Nominal charge or tastes.
Contact Information:	(813) 731-0615, travis@harmontampa.com, http://www.plantcity.org, Alternative contact: (813) 754-3707
Description:	Sample chocolate creations for nominal charge or buy confections to take home. Sponsored by Plant City Entertainment.

Flan Fest ~ *Great for Kids!*

City/County/Region:	Tampa / Hillsborough / Central West
Location:	Centennial Park, Ybor City, corner of 8th Ave. and 19th St.
General Date:	Last Saturday in February
Duration:	1 day
Year Started:	2004
Approx. Attendance:	Varies
Public Admission Fee:	Free
Other Fees/Costs:	Contest entry fee is free for both professional and amateur divisions.
Contact Information:	(813) 241-2442, ybormarket@yahoo.com, http://www.yborfreshmarket.citysearch.com
Description:	Amateur and professional flan contest with cash prizes. People's choice followed by celebrity judges casting votes for the best flan. Nominal charge for flan tasting. Live entertainment, dancing, flan eating contest, children's activities, shopping at the Ybor City Saturday Market. Hosted by the Ybor City Saturday Market and held in conjunction with Fiesta Day.

Great American Pie Festival ~ *Great for Kids!*

City/County/Region:	Orlando / Osceola / Central
Location:	Market Street, Celebration
General Date:	Last weekend in April
Duration:	2 days
Year Started:	2001
Approx. Attendance:	10,000
Public Admission Fee:	Free
Other Fees/Costs:	Admission to the 'Never Ending Pie Buffet' is $8 for adults, $6 for seniors 65+, $4 for children age 3-10 years old.

Contact Information: (847) 371-0170, apc@piecouncil.org, http://www.piecouncil.org/great.htm

Description: Featuring the never-ending pie buffet (fee required) with award winning pies, ice cream, toppings and beverages. Events include children's pie making, cooking demonstrations, children's games and crafts, pie eating contest, culinary demonstrations, APC Crisco® National Pie Championships®. Also other entertainment.

AN EVENING WITH EPIC CHEFS

City/County/Region: St. Augustine / St. Johns / Northeast
Location: Casa Monica Hotel, downtown St. Augustine
General Date: Last Thursday in April
Duration: 1 day
Year Started: 1995
Approx. Attendance: 200
Public Admission Fee: $$$
Other Fees/Costs: Ticket price $75 per person.
Contact Information: (904) 829-2273, epic@epiccommunityservices.org, http://www.epiccommunityservices.org
Description: An elegant four course dinner at the four star Casa Monica Hotel, downtown St. Augustine. Prepared by four of St. Augustine's premier chefs. Each Chef prepares their personal favorite. Silent and live auction and wine tasting included. Benefits EPIC Community Services.

TUPELO HONEY FESTIVAL ~ *Great for Kids!*

City/County/Region: Wewahitchka / Gulf / Northwest
Location: Lake Alice Park
General Date: 3rd Saturday in May
Duration: 1 day

7 - Miscellaneous Munchies

Year Started: 1993
Approx. Attendance: 4,000
Public Admission Fee: Free
Other Fees/Costs: Unavailable
Contact Information: (850) 639-5672, info@floridatupelohoney.com, http://www.floridatupelohoney.com/tupelofestival.cfm
Description: Honey festival hosted by Smiley Apiaries. Beekeepers are on hand to answer questions, as are local ag extension agents and 4-H Club members. Live entertainment, arts and crafts, face painting, horseback riding. And reminding everyone of why the festival exists, a giant yellow bumblebee passes out "honey sticks" of that sweet Tupelo Honey!

'I Like It Hot!' Festival & Barbecue

City/County/Region: Largo / Pinellas / Central West
Location: Minnreg Hall (Across from Honeywell), 6340 126th Avenue North
General Date: 3rd weekend in September
Duration: 2 days
Year Started: 2001
Approx. Attendance: 2,500
Public Admission Fee: $
Other Fees/Costs: Adult Admission is $3, kids 12 and under are free. Free parking.
Contact Information: (727) 423-8433, ilikeithotfestival@hotmail.com, http://www.ilikeithotfestival.com
Description: Sample and purchase hot and fiery foods and sauces along with a large variety of hot pepper plants. Take part in the pepper eating contest or the hot sauce and salsa competitions.

Chocolate Festival

City/County/Region: Coral Gables / Miami-Dade / Southeast
Location: Fairchild Tropical Botanic Garden, 10901 Old Cutler Road
General Date: Last weekend in October
Duration: 2 days
Year Started: 2006
Approx. Attendance: Varies
Public Admission Fee: $$
Other Fees/Costs: The event is free with admission to the Fairchild Tropical Botanic Garden: $20 for adults, $15 Senior citizens 65 and older, $10 for children 6 - 17, and free for Fairchild members and children 5 and under.
Contact Information: (305) 667-1651, pfernandez@fairchildgarden.org, http://www.fairchildgarden.org
Description: Learn, taste, and discover everything there is to know about chocolate and where it comes from! The event is free with admission to the Fairchild Tropical Botanic Garden.

Land O' Lakes Flapjack Festival ~ *Great for Kids!*

City/County/Region: Land O Lakes / Pasco / Central West
Location: Community Center property on Highway 41, 3 miles north of SR 54.
General Date: 1st full weekend in November
Duration: 3 days
Year Started: 1977
Approx. Attendance: 12,000
Public Admission Fee: Free
Other Fees/Costs: Free Flapjacks on Saturday from 8-10am. Nominal parking fee.

Contact Information: (813) 909-2722, office@centralpascochamber.com, http://www.centralpascochamber.com/?page=fjfest

Description: Free flapjacks on Saturday morning. Parade, flapjack eating contest, arts and crafts, entertainment, midway rides and activities. Sponsored by the Central Pasco Chamber of Commerce.

Death By Chocolate

City/County/Region: Largo / Pinellas / Central West
Location: Largo Cultural Center in Central Park, 105 Central Park Drive
General Date: 2nd Friday night in December
Duration: 1 day
Year Started: 1996
Approx. Attendance: 800
Public Admission Fee: $$
Other Fees/Costs: Tickets are $20 in advance and $25 at the door. Advance tickets are available at Main Street Chiropractic, online at Ticketmaster and at the Largo Cultural Center box office.
Contact Information: (727) 584-8821, info@largorotary.com, http://www.largorotary.com/Death%20By%20Chocolate.htm
Description: Features chocolate desserts from about twenty of the area's top chefs, caterers, and confectioners. Treats include truffles that look like snowballs, brownies soaked in coffee liqueur, and many other chocolate goodies! Fundraiser organized by the Rotary Club of Largo organizes to help raise money for the various community service programs and projects devoted to the children of Largo.

Cheesecake Challenge

City/County/Region:	St. Augustine / St. Johns / Northeast
Location:	Market Place, downtown St. Augustine
General Date:	2nd Saturday in December
Duration:	1 day
Year Started:	2002
Approx. Attendance:	300
Public Admission Fee:	Free
Other Fees/Costs:	Samples are $1 a piece, 6 for $5, or 12 for $10.
Contact Information:	(904) 829-2273, epic@epiccommunityservices.org, http://www.epiccommunityservices.org
Description:	Local restaurants compete for the honor of the "Best Cheesecake in St. Augustine." Patrons may purchase samples (small fee) of every cheesecake imaginable! Coffee and hot chocolate available. Live holiday music during the evening, downtown under the "Nights of Lights." Proceeds benefit Big Brother Big Sisters of St. Johns County.

8   Tantalizing Tastes

No matter what your favorite food is, "Taste Of" events are sure to please. Most have a wide assortment of local fare to satisfy varied palates. Sample bits of everything and have a sense of adventure—try some foods you've never tried before. Or latch onto your favorites. Your choice—and that's the point.

A chef puts his final touch on a signature dish.

Taste of Pine Island

City/County/Region: Pine Island / Lee / Southwest
Location: Phillips Park, St. James City
General Date: Last Sunday in January
Duration: 1 day
Year Started: Unavailable
Approx. Attendance: 2,500
Public Admission Fee: $
Other Fees/Costs: Requested donation is $5 at the gate, children ages 12 and under are admitted free.
Contact Information: (239) 283-0888, Info@pineislandchamber.org, http://www.pineislandchamber.org/events.html
Description: Various Island restaurants present their specialties to the general public. Music and vendors. Seafood chowder cook-off and the annual "Fish Drop" fund-raiser for the Kiwanis Scholarship Fund. Sponsored by the Kiwanis Club of Greater Pine Island.

Taste of the Beach (Lauderdale-By-The-Sea)

City/County/Region: Lauderdale-By-The-Sea / Broward / Southeast
Location: El Mar & El Prado, one block east of A1A and one block north of Commercial Boulevard.
General Date: Last Wednesday in February
Duration: 1 day
Year Started: 2001
Approx. Attendance: 600
Public Admission Fee: $$
Other Fees/Costs: Tickets are $30.
Contact Information: (954) 776-1000, info@lbts.com, http://www.lbts.com

8 - Tantalizing Tastes

Description: Join the fun (rain or shine) under the tent for food, drink, entertainment, silent auction—something for everyone. Please your palate by trying the best offerings from 40 of the finest local restaurants. Lots of variety, from cookies to canapés, sushi to scampi. Drinks are also included in the admission fee. Sponsored by the Lauderdale-By-The-Sea Chamber of Commerce with proceeds benefiting the LBTS Chamber of Commerce and a portion awarded to the Culinary School at the Art Institute of Ft. Lauderdale for the education of one of their talented students. Casual dress.

TASTE OF KEY WEST

City/County/Region: Key West / Monroe / Southwest
Location: Truman Annex at the end of Southard Street
General Date: 3rd Monday in April
Duration: 1 day
Year Started: 1996
Approx. Attendance: 5,000
Public Admission Fee: Free
Other Fees/Costs: Food and wine tickets cost $1 each with "tastes" ranging from $3 to $8. The Commemorative Wine Glasses sell for $6 each. Participants can arrive an hour early to purchase their glasses and tickets prior to the gates opening. Free parking.
Contact Information: (305) 296-6196, pam.d@aidshelp.cc, http://www.aidshelp.cc
Description: Benefits the Key West AIDS Help Inc. The gourmet gala features delicacies from local restaurants as well as vintages from several wineries.

A Taste of St. Augustine ~ *Great for Kids!*

City/County/Region: St. Augustine / St. Johns / Northeast
Location: Francis Field, downtown St. Augustine
General Date: Last Saturday in April
Duration: 1 day
Year Started: 1995
Approx. Attendance: 5,000
Public Admission Fee: $
Other Fees/Costs: Admission $2 per person.
Contact Information: (904) 829-2273, epic@epiccommunityservices.org, http://www.epiccommunityservices.org
Description: Over thirty local restaurants compete for the prestigious Taste of St. Augustine (TOStA) Awards. Ethinic, upscale, seafood, family dining, and more! Kid's area with moonwalk and other fun for children. Beer and wine served. Live music all day! Benefits EPIC Community Services non-profit organization.

A Taste of the Coast An Artful Affair

City/County/Region: Port Saint Joe / Gulf / Northwest
Location: The Centennial Building
General Date: Last Saturday in April
Duration: 1 day
Year Started: 2004
Approx. Attendance: Varies
Public Admission Fee: $$
Other Fees/Costs: Admission is $30. Admission to the Preview Party the night before is an additional $10 for those who have purchased the main event ticket. There are no sales to attend only the Preview Party.

Contact Information: (850) 227-1223, Sandra@gulfchamber.org, http://www.atasteofthecoast.com, Toll free number for the Gulf County Chamber of Commerce is (800) 239-9553, http://www.gulfchamber.org

Description: Local restaurants showcase delectable samplings of the freshest seafood, fun appetizers and taste tempting desserts in café settings. Event also showcases regional artists (original paintings, autographed prints, and award-winning photography) and authors. Silent and live auctions, live music, and wine bar. Preview Party the night before (additional admission fee required) gives ticket holders an opportunity to mingle and talk with the artists who are donate their work to this event. Proceeds benefit the Gulf County Scholarship Program and the Gulf County Chamber's "Independence on the Coast" celebration.

TASTE OF THE ISLANDS

City/County/Region: Sanibel / Lee / Southwest
Location: Sanibel Community Park, Periwinkle Way
General Date: In April or early May
Duration: 1 day
Year Started: 1980
Approx. Attendance: 3,500
Public Admission Fee: $
Other Fees/Costs: Admission $5, food and beverage tickets $1 each.
Contact Information: (239) 472-3644, crowclinic@aol.com, http://www.crowclinic.org/events.cfm
Description: Day of tasting with many of Sanibel and Captiva's most popular restaurants and terrific

bands to entertain you throughout the day. Arrive early, as some of the favorite foods may run out toward the end of the event! Benefit for the Clinic for the Rehabilitation of Wildlife, Inc.

Taste of Collier

City/County/Region: Naples / Collier / Southwest
Location: Olde Naples on Third Street
General Date: 1st Sunday in May
Duration: 1 day
Year Started: 1984
Approx. Attendance: 8,000
Public Admission Fee: $
Other Fees/Costs: Admission is $4 per person, children 10 and under are free. Tasting portions from each restaurant range from $1 to $3 per portion.
Contact Information: (239) 272-1907, info@tasteofcollier.org, http://www.tasteofcollier.org
Description: Live performances by area bands, Waiter/Waitress games, ice-carving contest, and of course, lots of wonderful food! Hosted by the Collier County Chapter of the Florida Restaurant Association and benefits local non-profit organizations.

Taste of Mount Dora

City/County/Region: Mount Dora / Lake / Central
Location: Mount Dora Chamber of Commerce lawn, 341 N. Alexander Street
General Date: 1st Sunday in May
Duration: 1 day

8 - Tantalizing Tastes

Year Started: 2001
Approx. Attendance: 800
Public Admission Fee: $$
Other Fees/Costs: Tickets go on sale March 1st at the Mount Dora Area Chamber of Commerce and are $30 in advance or $35 the day of event. Get tickets early because the event usually sells out.
Contact Information: (352) 383-2165, chamber@mountdora.com, http://www.mountdora.com
Description: Presented by the Mount Dora Area Chamber of Commerce. Culinary delights prepared by Mount Dora's finest restaurants and beautifully decorated booths.

TASTE OF BOYNTON

City/County/Region: Boynton Beach / Palm Beach / Southeast
Location: Westchester Country Club, 12250 Westchester Club Dr.
General Date: 1st or 2nd Friday in June
Duration: 1 day
Year Started: Unavailable
Approx. Attendance: 350
Public Admission Fee: $$$
Other Fees/Costs: Tickets are $40 in advance through the Greater Boynton Beach Chamber of Commerce. No tickets sold at the door.
Contact Information: (561) 732-9501, chamber@boyntonbeach.org, http://www.tasteofboynton.com
Description: Presented by the Greater Boynton Beach Chamber of Commerce. Chamber-member restaurants participate and give samplings of food. In addition to the great food, there's a

141

wine tasting with over 150 different wines, a silent auction, and live entertainment for dancing the night away! No one under 21 is admitted.

TASTE OF PINELLAS ~ *Great for Kids!*

City/County/Region: St. Petersburg / Pinellas / Central West
Location: Vinoy Park, Fifth Avenue NE and Bayshore Drive
General Date: 1st weekend in June
Duration: 3 days
Year Started: 1986
Approx. Attendance: 100,000
Public Admission Fee: Free
Other Fees/Costs: Fee for tastes from $1-$4 each.
Contact Information: (727) 579-2026, info@allkids.org, http://www.allkids.org/support/taste, Alternative contact: All Children's Hospital, (727) 898-7451
Description: Tastes from 50 plus area restaurants, national act concerts, kid's area, celebrity chef cooking theater and fireworks. Benefits All Children's Hospital.

FORT MYERS TASTE OF THE BEACH ~ *Great for Kids!*

City/County/Region: Fort Myers Beach / Lee / Southwest
Location: Old San Carlos Blvd.
General Date: 1st Sunday in June
Duration: 1 day
Year Started: 1996
Approx. Attendance: 4,000

8 - Tantalizing Tastes

Public Admission Fee:	$
Other Fees/Costs:	Admission Fee is $3.
Contact Information:	(239) 454-7500, info@fmbchamber.com, http://www.fmbchamber.com
Description:	Featuring seafood, ribs, and desserts. Waiter/waitress contest, games for kids, entertainment, and raffles. Sponsored by the Fort Myers Beach Chamber of Commerce.

Taste of Weston

City/County/Region:	Fort Lauderdale / Broward / Southeast
Location:	Wyndham Bonaventure Resort & Spa, 250 Racquet Club Rd.
General Date:	2nd Wednesday in September
Duration:	1 day
Year Started:	2001
Approx. Attendance:	700
Public Admission Fee:	$$$
Other Fees/Costs:	Admission is $45 at door, $35 prepaid.
Contact Information:	(954) 660-0601, Info@WestonFloridaChamber.com, http://www.westonfloridachamber.com, Alternative contact: Fort Lauderdale Chamber of Commerce, http://www.ftlchamber.com
Description:	Weston's signature professional event of the year featuring over 30 wine and food booths set up in the Grand Ballroom. Sample West Broward's finest cuisine prepared by professionals from Weston and West Broward. Wine and spirits tasting provided by The Grape Merchant. Music entertainment. A portion of the proceeds will benefit Weston YMCA and Boys & Girls Clubs.

Taste of Clearwater

City/County/Region: Clearwater / Pinellas / Central West
Location: Harborview Center, 300 Cleveland St.
General Date: 3rd Tuesday in September
Duration: 1 day
Year Started: 1990
Approx. Attendance: 3,800
Public Admission Fee: $$
Other Fees/Costs: Tickets are $18 in advance or $22 at the door.
Contact Information: (727) 461-0011, kbrown@clearwaterflorida.org, http://www.ClearwaterFlorida.org
Description: Pay one price and sample fares from over 50 Bay area restaurants. Once you are indoors (and air-conditioned!), everything is free. It's the Ultimate Buffet from some of the Bay areas finest restaurants. Vote for your favorites ("Best of Taste" and "Best Themed Booth") before you leave. Also includes free beer, wine, water, and soda samples. Entertainment throughout the event featuring Jazz on the Main Stage, solo artist, a caricature artist, roaming magician and much more. A huge "Chinese Raffle" includes dozens of gift baskets to be won. Discount if you purchase tickets in advance instead of at the door.

Taste of Plant City ~ *Great for Kids!*

City/County/Region: Plant City / Pinellas / Central West
Location: Plant City Stadium, 1810 E Park Road
General Date: 3rd Saturday in October
Duration: 1 day

8 - Tantalizing Tastes

Year Started:	Unavailable
Approx. Attendance:	Varies
Public Admission Fee:	$$
Other Fees/Costs:	Tickets are $25.
Contact Information:	(813) 764-0625, unitedfoodbank.ofplantcity@verizon.net, http://www.plantcity.org, Alternative contact: Greater Plant City Chamber of Commerce, (813) 754-3707, info@plantcity.org, http://www.plantcitychamber.org
Description:	Local restaurants offer samplings, plus live music and family activities. Proceeds benefit United Food Bank.

TASTE AT BAY STREET ~ *Great for Kids!*

City/County/Region:	Tampa / Hillsborough / Central West
Location:	International Plaza
General Date:	2nd weekend in October
Duration:	3 days
Year Started:	2002
Approx. Attendance:	10,000
Public Admission Fee:	Free
Other Fees/Costs:	Taste ticket prices start at $2.
Contact Information:	(813) 342-3790, http://www.shopinternationalplaza.com
Description:	Three-day indoor/outdoor event of food, wine, spirits, live music, and children's entertainment Over 15 restaurants and 80 international taste selections for a small fee. Benefits local charities.

Taste of Gulfport

City/County/Region:	Gulfport / Pinellas / Central West
Location:	Beach Blvd in the heart of Gulfport's Historic Waterfront District
General Date:	1st Saturday in November
Duration:	1 day
Year Started:	2004
Approx. Attendance:	6,000
Public Admission Fee:	Free
Other Fees/Costs:	Nominal fee for tastes.
Contact Information:	(727) 344-3711, gulfport.chamberofcommerce@verizon.net, http://www.gulfportchamberofcommerce.com
Description:	Menu items from local restaurants. Includes free entertainment all day on main stage and the restaurants and bars on Beach Blvd. Festival coincides with an adjacent Antique Auto Show at Clymer Park. A full day of events! Sponsored by the Gulfport Chamber of Commerce.

Taste of Manatee ~ *Great for Kids!*

City/County/Region:	Bradenton / Manatee / Central West
Location:	Barcarrotta Blvd., Downtown
General Date:	1st weekend in November
Duration:	2 days
Year Started:	1986
Approx. Attendance:	7,000
Public Admission Fee:	Free
Other Fees/Costs:	Unavailable

Contact Information: (941) 747-4655, Info@mealsonwheelsplus.org, http://www.mowplus.org/events.html

Description: Benefits Meals on Wheels Plus. Twenty plus restaurants, arts and crafts, kids games, music and a sports bar with TV's to watch the Bucs Game. Located on the beautiful Manatee River.

ZOOFARI

City/County/Region: Tampa / Hillsborough / Central West
Location: Tampa's Lowry Park Zoo
General Date: 1st Saturday in November
Duration: 1 day
Year Started: 1987
Approx. Attendance: 4,400
Public Admission Fee: $$$
Other Fees/Costs: Tickets prices may change from year to year, so confirm with Lowry Park Zoo.
Contact Information: (813) 935-8552, information@lowryparkzoo.com, http://www.lowryparkzoo.com
Description: Known as one of the largest and "wildest" all-inclusive food festivals in the Tampa Bay Area, Lowry Park Zoo invites food lovers to its annual Zoofari feeding frenzy. Featuring great food sampling from more than 80 restaurants, open bar, live music and Art Safari—the art auction that's king in the animal kingdom. Zoofari general admission tickets are all-inclusive. VIP/Group packages are available in the exclusive "Rhino Club."

Fort Myers Taste of the Town - *Great for Kids!*

City/County/Region:	Fort Myers / Lee / Southwest
Location:	Centennial Park
General Date:	1st Sunday in November
Duration:	1 day
Year Started:	1983
Approx. Attendance:	16,000
Public Admission Fee:	$
Other Fees/Costs:	Tickets $4 in advance, $5 at the door.
Contact Information:	(239) 277-1197, juniorleaguefm@aol.com, http://www.jlfm.org
Description:	Features samplings from more than 40 local restaurants. Live music and children's entertainment. Sponsored by the Junior League of Fort Myers.

A   Directory by Region

Appendix A lists each festival by region. A statewide Florida map depicts the North, Central, and South regions. Each section is preceded by a regional map which shows sub-regions and county boundaries. The festivals are sorted by city and event name under each region's heading. The city where the festival is held is indicated next to the event name.

Map 1: Florida Regional Map

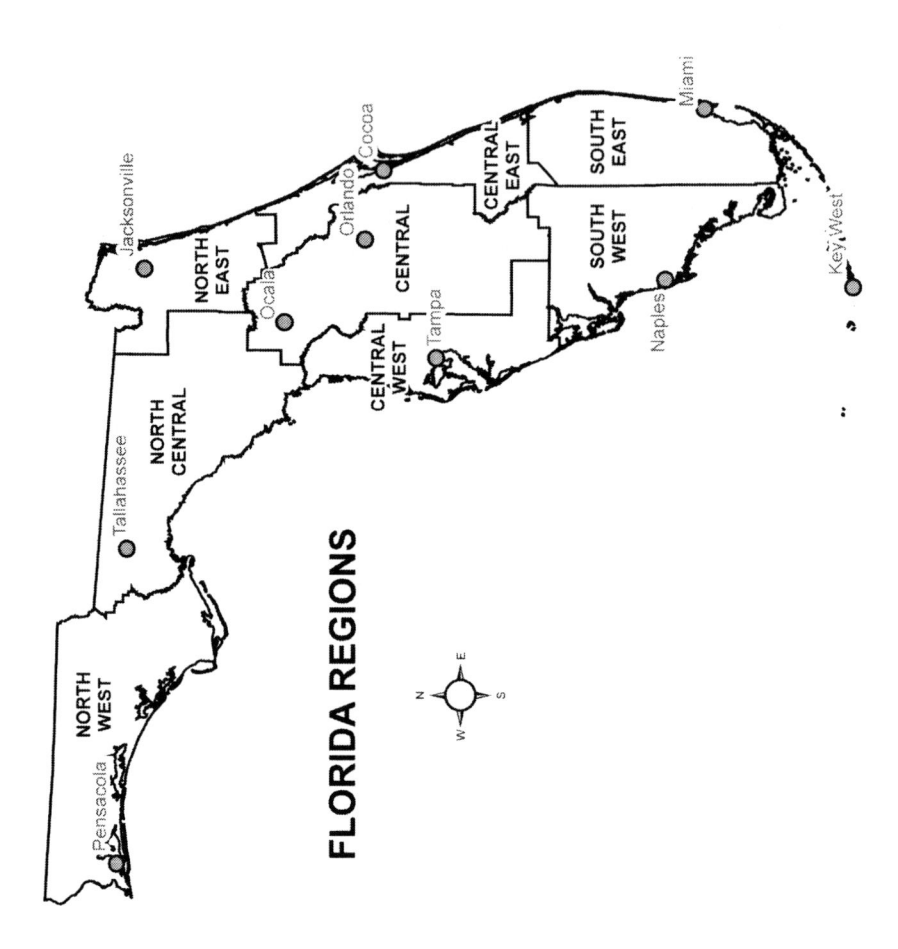

A - Directory by Region

Map 2: North Regions

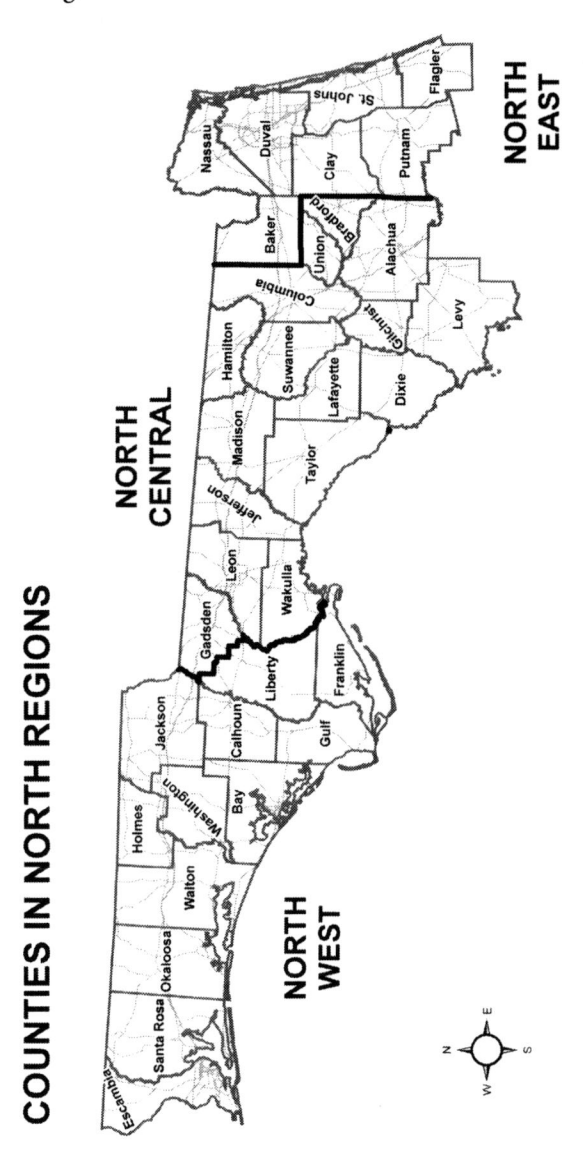

Food Fest! Your Complete Guide to Florida's Food Festivals

Northwest

Festival - City	Page
Florida Seafood Festival - Apalachicola	39
Panhandle Watermelon Festival - Chipley	94
Destin Seafood Festival - Destin	33
Gulf Coast Regional Chili Cookoff - Eastpoint	56
Gabbert Farm Peanut Festival - Jay	105
Boggy Barbecue Cookoff - Niceville	66
Boggy Bayou Mullet Festival - Niceville	35
Fall Seafood and Pirate Fest - Panama City	31
National Shrimp and Oyster Festival - Panama City	21
Indian Summer Seafood Festival - Panama City Beach	34
'Do It At The Line' Super Chili Bowl Cookoff - Pensacola	51
Beulah Sausage Festival - Pensacola	61
Emerald Coast Brew Fest & Beach Party - Pensacola	122
Pensacola Crawfish Creole Fiesta - Pensacola	24
Pensacola Seafood Festival - Pensacola	32
A Taste of the Coast An Artful Affair - Port Saint Joe	138
Gulf County Scallop Festival - Port Saint Joe	29
Great Southern Gumbo Cook-off - Sandestin	45
Sandestin Wine Festival - Sandestin	115
Seafood & Mini Wine Fest - Sandestin	29
Tupelo Honey Festival - Wewahitchka	130

North Central

Festival - City	Page
Cedar Key Seafood Festival - Cedar Key	36
Clamerica Celebration - Cedar Key	28
Chiefland Watermelon Festival - Chiefland	90
Windsor Zucchini Festival - Gainesville	103
Hog Wild and Pig Crazy Barbecue Cook-off - Lake City	64
Jefferson County Watermelon Festival - Monticello	92

Festival - City	Page
Newberry Watermelon Festival - Newberry	90
Panacea Blue Crab Festival - Panacea	25
Beefcember Fest - Starke	81
Bradford County Strawberry Festival - Starke	88
Florida Wine Festival - Tallahassee	113
Tallahassee Wine and Food Festival - Tallahassee	124
Wellborn Blueberry Festival - Wellborn	91
Central Florida Peanut Festival - Williston	104

NORTHEAST

Festival - City	Page
Bostwick Blueberry Festival - Bostwick	93
Northeast Florida Blueberries & Barbecue Festival - Callahan	92
St. Johns River Catfish Festival - Crescent City	19
Isle Of Eight Flags Shrimp Festival - Fernandina Beach	24
First Coast Ham Jam - Green Cove Springs	79
'Make it Mild or Make it Wild' Chili Cook-off - Jacksonville	65
Backyard BBQ Blast - Jacksonville	62
Folio Weekly Beer & Music Festival - Jacksonville	120
Great Atlantic Seafood Festival - Jacksonville	16
Palatka Blue Crab Festival - Palatka	27
A Taste of St. Augustine - St. Augustine	138
An Evening with EPIC Chefs - St. Augustine	130
Cheesecake Challenge - St. Augustine	134
Rhythm and Ribs Festival - St. Augustine	67
San Sebastian Harvest Festival & Grape Stomp - St. Augustine	121
San Sebastian Winefest - St. Augustine	110
St. Augustine Lions Seafood Festival - St. Augustine	18

Food Fest! Your Complete Guide to Florida's Food Festivals

Map 3: Central Regions

COUNTIES IN CENTRAL REGIONS

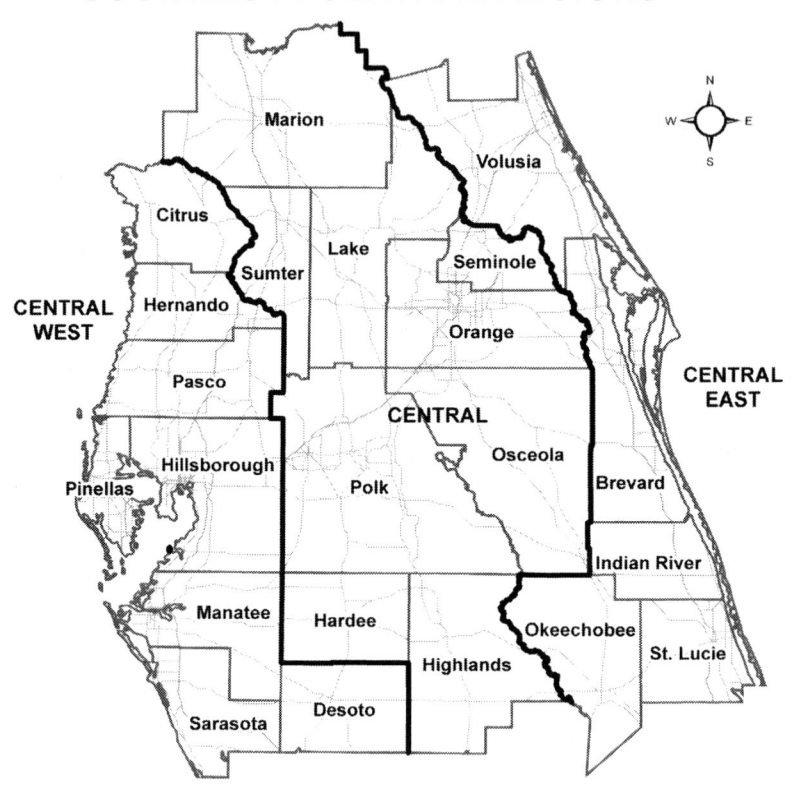

A - Directory by Region

CENTRAL WEST

Festival - City	Page
Arcadia Watermelon Festival - Arcadia	89
DeSoto County Watermelon Festival - Arcadia	89
Hunsader Farms Pumpkin Festival - Bradenton	106
Taste of Manatee - Bradenton	146
Hernando County BBQ & Rodeo Festival - Brooksville	74
Taste of Clearwater - Clearwater	144
Frenchy's Stone Crab Festival - Clearwater Beach	38
Cortez Commercial Fishing Festival - Cortez	11
Florida Barbecue Association Funcook - Crystal River	72
Kumquat Festival - Dade City	84
Dunedin Wines the Blues - Dunedin	125
Englewood Beach / Burr Smidt Memorial Chili Cookoff - Englewood	63
Florida Sunshine Pod Cookoff - Englewood	64
Floral City Strawberry Festival - Floral City	87
Taste of Gulfport - Gulfport	146
Hernando Beach Seafood Festival - Hernando Beach	34
Southeast Chili Cookoff - Homosassa	75
Waterfront Chili Cookoff - Homosassa	76
Hudson Seafest - Hudson	41
Land O' Lakes Flapjack Festival - Land O' Lakes	132
'I Like It Hot!' Festival & Barbecue - Largo	131
Battle of the Badges - Largo	68
Death By Chocolate - Largo	133
Stone Crab, Seafood, and Wine Festival - Longboat Key	37
John's Pass Seafood Festival - Madeira Beach	39
Cotee River Seafood Festival and Boat Show - New Port Richey	26
Fine Wine & Food Festival - Oldsmar	123
Cajun Cafe on the Bayou Crawfish Festival - Pinellas Park	20
Chili Blaze - Pinellas Park	62
Florida Strawberry Festival - Plant City	86

157

Festival - City	Page
Plant City Arts Council Chili Cookoff - Plant City	54
Plant City Pig Jam - Plant City	80
Taste of Chocolate Festival - Plant City	128
Taste of Plant City - Plant City	144
Spring Jubilee Chili Cook-off - Riverview	67
Ruskin Seafood Festival - Ruskin	40
Ruskin Tomato Festival - Ruskin	102
Harbor Sounds Seafood & Music Festival - Safety Harbor	12
Safety Harbor Wine Festival - Safety Harbor	125
Florida Winefest & Auction - Sarasota	116
Sun-N-Fun RV Resort Chili Cookoff - Sarasota	71
Cajun Zydeco Crawfish Festival - St. Petersburg	13
Jim's Chili Cookoff - St. Petersburg	45
Ribfest - St. Petersburg	79
Taste of Pinellas - St. Petersburg	142
BBQfest - Tampa	70
Bern's Winefest - Tampa	116
Denning's Lounge Chili Cookoff - Tampa	63
Einstein on Wine - Tampa	108
Flan Fest - Tampa	129
Florida Brewers Guild BeerFest - Tampa	111
Great Northwest Rib & Family Fest - Tampa	50
Taste at Bay Street - Tampa	145
WaZoo - Tampa	121
Zoofari - Tampa	147
Gavel & Grapes Festival - Tarpon Springs	120
Leepa-Rattner Museum of Art Stone Crab Fest - Tarpon Springs	36
Suncoast Chili Cookoff - Tarpon Springs	47

A - Directory by Region

CENTRAL

Festival - City	Page
Astor Chamber Of Commerce Chili Cook-off - Astor	58
Bluegrass & BBQ Festival - Auburndale	60
Belleview Chili Cook-off - Belleview	76
Lakeridge Winefest - Clermont	109
Pig on the Pond - Clermont	57
Sunshine Regional Chili Cook-Off - Kissimmee	46
Lakeland Pig Festival - Lakeland	48
Leesburg Chili Cook-Off - Leesburg	78
Spring Fish Fry - Leesburg	20
Minneola Fall Fest BBQ Contest - Minneola	73
Taste of Mount Dora - Mount Dora	140
Mulberry Fine Swine At The Pit - Mulberry	73
Marion County Chili Cook-Off - Ocala	74
Epcot Food and Wine Festival - Orlando	123
Florida Cracker Oyster Festival - Orlando	32
Great American Pie Festival - Orlando	129
Orlando Beer Festival - Orlando	126
Rajuncajun Crawfish Festival - Orlando	21
Cactus Jack's Chili Cookoff - Salt Springs	59
Central Florida BBQ Festival - Sebring	44
Smoke 'n Blues BBQ - St. Cloud	69
Firefight at Spanish Springs - The Villages	52
Grillin & Chillin on Main Wauchula - Wauchula	50
'Smoke on the Water' BBQ - Winter Haven	53
Florida Citrus Festival - Winter Haven	84
Police, Firefighter, & EMS Chili Cook Off - Winter Haven	49
Zellwood Sweet Corn Festival - Zellwood	104

Central East

Festival - City	Page
Daytona Beach Bayou Boil - Daytona Beach	26
Shores Wine and Food Festival - Daytona Beach	118
DeLand Wild Game Feast - De Land	68
Great Bowls of Fire Chili Cookoff - De Land	77
Fellsmere Frog Leg Festival - Fellsmere	46
Grant Seafood Festival - Grant	11
Q-Fest BBQ & Music Festival - Grant	72
Jumbalaya Jam - Melbourne	10
Speckled Perch Festival - Okeechobee	14
Top Of The Lake BBQ Affair - Okeechobee	56
The Big Squeeze - Palm Bay	88
Shrimp Fest - Ponce Inlet	22
Sebastian Clambake Lagoon Festival - Sebastian	30
Titusville Sunrise Rotary Club Chili Cookoff - Titusville	52
Indian River County Firefighters' Chili Cookoff - Vero Beach	70

A - Directory by Region

Map 4: South Regions

COUNTIES IN SOUTH REGIONS

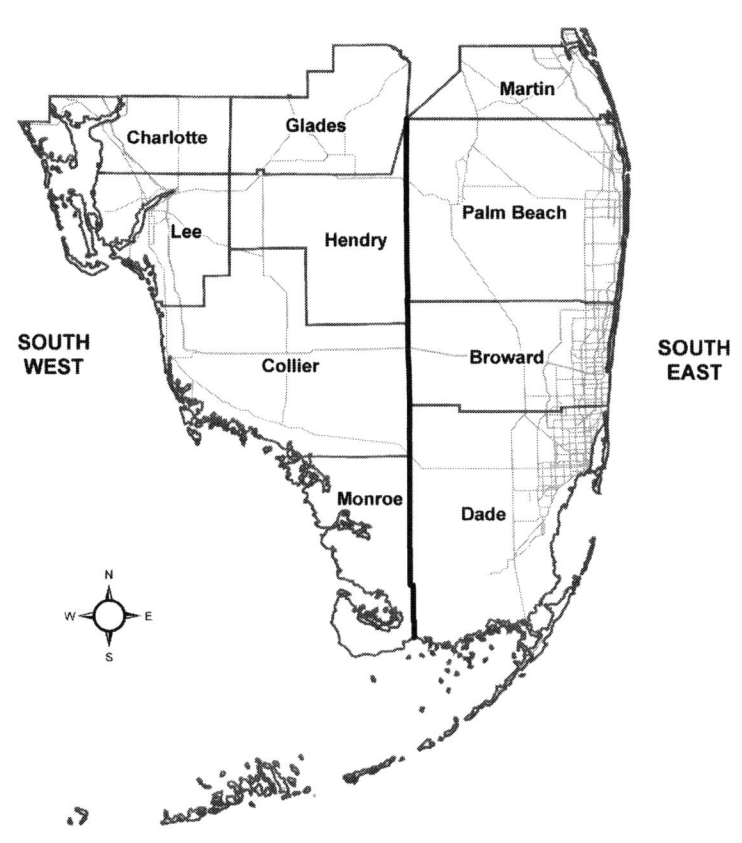

Southwest

Festival - City	Page
Celebrate Bonita District Chili Cookoff - Bonita Springs	66
Buckhead Ridge Catfish Festival - Buckhead Ridge	8
Sugar Festival - Clewiston	101
Estero High Key Club Chili Cookoff - Estero	55
Everglades Seafood Festival - Everglades	10
Fort Myers Taste of the Town - Fort Myers	148
Fort Myers Beach Shrimp Festival - Fort Myers Beach	14
Fort Myers Taste Of The Beach - Fort Myers Beach	142
Florida Keys Regional Cookoff - Key Largo	55
Florida Keys Seafood Festival - Key West	9
Florida Keys Tropical Fruit Fiesta - Key West	95
Key West Food and Wine Festival - Key West	119
Taste of Key West - Key West	137
Honey Festival - La Belle	128
Swamp Cabbage Festival - La Belle	100
Sour Orange Festival - Lakeport	85
Marathon Seafood Festival - Marathon	16
Goodland Mullet Festival - Marco Island	8
Naples Country Jam Chili Cookoff - Naples	60
Naples Winter Wine Festival - Naples	108
Taste of Collier - Naples	140
Mangomania Tropical Fruit Fair - Pine Island	96
Taste of Pine Island - Pine Island	136
Placida Rotary Seafood Festival - Placida	17
Taste of the Islands - Sanibel	139
Stone Crab Fest - Summerland Key	37

A - Directory by Region

Southeast

Festival - City	Page
Boca Bacchanal Winefest - Boca Raton	112
Taste of Boynton - Boynton Beach	141
Biltmore International Food & Wine Weekend - Coral Gables	117
Chocolate Festival - Coral Gables	132
Coral Gables Wine & Food Festival - Coral Gables	114
International Mango Festival - Coral Gables	94
Delray Beach Garlic Fest - Delray Beach	100
Las Olas Wine and Food Festival - Fort Lauderdale	118
New Times Beerfest - Fort Lauderdale	114
Taste of Weston - Fort Lauderdale	143
Hollywood Beach Clambake - Hollywood	30
Jensen Beach Pineapple Festival - Jensen Beach	96
Palm Beach County Firefighters/Paramedics M.D.A. Chili Cookoff - Lake Worth	78
Taste of the Beach (Lauderdale-By-The-Sea) - Lauderdale-By-The-Sea	136
Miami Wine and Food Festival - Miami	112
South Beach Wine and Food Festival - Miami	110
Cajun Blues Crawfish Festival - Palm Beach	18
Palm Beach Seafood Festival - Palm Beach	15
99.9 Kiss Country Regional Chili Cookoff - Pembroke Pines	48
Chili in the Village Regional Cookoff - Pinecrest	54
Pompano Beach Seafood Festival - Pompano Beach	23
Sweet Corn Fiesta - West Palm Beach	102
Hospice Chili Cookoff - Wilton Manors	77

163

B   Directory by Month

Appendix B lists each festival by month. The festivals are sorted by city and event name under each month's heading. The city where the festival is held is indicated next to the event name.

Food Fest! Your Complete Guide to Florida's Food Festivals

January

Festival - City	Page
Buckhead Ridge Catfish Festival - Buckhead Ridge	8
Kumquat Festival - Dade City	84
Fellsmere Frog Leg Festival - Fellsmere	46
Florida Keys Seafood Festival - Key West	9
Sunshine Regional Chili Cook-Off - Kissimmee	46
Honey Festival - La Belle	128
Lakeland Pig Festival - Lakeland	48
Goodland Mullet Festival - Marco Island	8
Naples Winter Wine Festival - Naples	108
99.9 Kiss Country Regional Chili Cookoff - Pembroke Pines	48
Taste of Pine Island - Pine Island	136
Great Southern Gumbo Cook-off - Sandestin	45
Central Florida BBQ Festival - Sebring	44
Jim's Chili Cookoff - St. Petersburg	45
Suncoast Chili Cookoff - Tarpon Springs	47
Florida Citrus Festival - Winter Haven	84
Police, Firefighter, & EMS Chili Cook Off - Winter Haven	49

February

Festival - City	Page
Lakeridge Winefest - Clermont	109
Cortez Commercial Fishing Festival - Cortez	11
Delray Beach Garlic Fest - Delray Beach	100
Estero High Key Club Chili Cookoff - Estero	55
Everglades Seafood Festival - Everglades	10
Grant Seafood Festival - Grant	11
Florida Keys Regional Cookoff - Key Largo	55
Swamp Cabbage Festival - La Belle	100
Sour Orange Festival - Lakeport	85

Festival - City	Page
Taste of the Beach (Lauderdale-By-The-Sea) - Lauderdale-By-The-Sea	136
Jumbalaya Jam - Melbourne	10
South Beach Wine and Food Festival - Miami	110
'Do It At The Line' Super Chili Bowl Cookoff - Pensacola	51
Chili in the Village Regional Cookoff - Pinecrest	54
Plant City Arts Council Chili Cookoff - Plant City	54
Taste of Chocolate Festival - Plant City	128
San Sebastian Winefest - St. Augustine	110
Einstein on Wine - Tampa	108
Flan Fest - Tampa	129
Great Northwest Rib & Family Fest - Tampa	50
Firefight at Spanish Springs - The Villages	52
Titusville Sunrise Rotary Club Chili Cookoff - Titusville	52
Grillin & Chillin on Main Wauchula - Wauchula	50
'Smoke on the Water' BBQ - Winter Haven	53

MARCH

Festival - City	Page
Astor Chamber Of Commerce Chili Cook-off - Astor	58
Bluegrass & BBQ Festival - Auburndale	60
Boca Bacchanal Winefest - Boca Raton	112
Pig on the Pond - Clermont	57
Gulf Coast Regional Chili Cookoff - Eastpoint	56
Englewood Beach / Burr Smidt Memorial Chili Cookoff - Englewood	63
Florida Sunshine Pod Cookoff - Englewood	64
Floral City Strawberry Festival - Floral City	87
Fort Myers Beach Shrimp Festival - Fort Myers Beach	14
Backyard BBQ Blast - Jacksonville	62
Great Atlantic Seafood Festival - Jacksonville	16
Marathon Seafood Festival - Marathon	16

Festival - City	Page
Miami Wine and Food Festival - Miami	112
Naples Country Jam Chili Cookoff - Naples	60
Speckled Perch Festival - Okeechobee	14
Top Of The Lake BBQ Affair - Okeechobee	56
Palm Beach Seafood Festival - Palm Beach	15
Beulah Sausage Festival - Pensacola	61
Chili Blaze - Pinellas Park	62
Placida Rotary Seafood Festival - Placida	17
Florida Strawberry Festival - Plant City	86
Harbor Sounds Seafood & Music Festival - Safety Harbor	12
Cactus Jack's Chili Cookoff - Salt Springs	59
St. Augustine Lions Seafood Festival - St. Augustine	18
Cajun Zydeco Crawfish Festival - St. Petersburg	13
Denning's Lounge Chili Cookoff - Tampa	63
Florida Brewers Guild BeerFest - Tampa	111

APRIL

Festival - City	Page
Celebrate Bonita District Chili Cookoff - Bonita Springs	66
Sugar Festival - Clewiston	101
Coral Gables Wine & Food Festival - Coral Gables	114
St. Johns River Catfish Festival - Crescent City	19
New Times Beerfest - Fort Lauderdale	114
'Make it Mild or Make it Wild' Chili Cook-off - Jacksonville	65
Taste of Key West - Key West	137
Hog Wild and Pig Crazy Barbecue Cook-off - Lake City	64
Spring Fish Fry - Leesburg	20
Boggy Barbecue Cookoff - Niceville	66
Great American Pie Festival - Orlando	129
Rajuncajun Crawfish Festival - Orlando	21
The Big Squeeze - Palm Bay	88
Cajun Blues Crawfish Festival - Palm Beach	18

Festival - City	Page
National Shrimp and Oyster Festival - Panama City	21
Cajun Cafe on the Bayou Crawfish Festival - Pinellas Park	20
Pompano Beach Seafood Festival - Pompano Beach	23
Shrimp Fest - Ponce Inlet	22
A Taste of the Coast An Artful Affair - Port Saint Joe	138
Spring Jubilee Chili Cook-off - Riverview	67
Sandestin Wine Festival - Sandestin	115
Taste of the Islands - Sanibel	139
Florida Winefest & Auction - Sarasota	116
A Taste of St. Augustine - St. Augustine	138
An Evening with EPIC Chefs - St. Augustine	130
Rhythm and Ribs Festival - St. Augustine	67
Bradford County Strawberry Festival - Starke	88
Florida Wine Festival - Tallahassee	113
Bern's Winefest - Tampa	116
Sweet Corn Fiesta - West Palm Beach	102

May

Festival - City	Page
Arcadia Watermelon Festival - Arcadia	89
DeSoto County Watermelon Festival - Arcadia	89
Biltmore International Food & Wine Weekend - Coral Gables	117
Daytona Beach Bayou Boil - Daytona Beach	26
DeLand Wild Game Feast - De Land	68
Isle Of Eight Flags Shrimp Festival - Fernandina Beach	24
Las Olas Wine and Food Festival - Fort Lauderdale	118
Windsor Zucchini Festival - Gainesville	103
Battle of the Badges - Largo	68
Taste of Mount Dora - Mount Dora	140
Taste of Collier - Naples	140
Cotee River Seafood Festival and Boat Show - New Port Richey	26

Food Fest! Your Complete Guide to Florida's Food Festivals

Festival - City	Page
Newberry Watermelon Festival - Newberry	90
Palatka Blue Crab Festival - Palatka	27
Panacea Blue Crab Festival - Panacea	25
Pensacola Crawfish Creole Fiesta - Pensacola	24
Ruskin Tomato Festival - Ruskin	102
Smoke 'n Blues BBQ - St. Cloud	69
BBQfest - Tampa	70
Indian River County Firefighters' Chili Cookoff - Vero Beach	70
Tupelo Honey Festival - Wewahitchka	130
Zellwood Sweet Corn Festival - Zellwood	104

JUNE

Festival - City	Page
Bostwick Blueberry Festival - Bostwick	93
Taste of Boynton - Boynton Beach	141
Northeast Florida Blueberries & Barbecue Festival - Callahan	92
Chiefland Watermelon Festival - Chiefland	90
Panhandle Watermelon Festival - Chipley	94
Shores Wine and Food Festival - Daytona Beach	118
Fort Myers Taste Of The Beach - Fort Myers Beach	142
Jefferson County Watermelon Festival - Monticello	92
Taste of Pinellas - St. Petersburg	142
Wellborn Blueberry Festival - Wellborn	91

JULY

Festival - City	Page
Clamerica Celebration - Cedar Key	28
International Mango Festival - Coral Gables	94
Folio Weekly Beer & Music Festival - Jacksonville	120
Florida Keys Tropical Fruit Fiesta - Key West	95
Key West Food and Wine Festival - Key West	119

Festival - City	Page
Mangomania Tropical Fruit Fair - Pine Island	96
Gavel & Grapes Festival - Tarpon Springs	120

August

Festival - City	Page
Gulf County Scallop Festival - Port Saint Joe	29
San Sebastian Harvest Festival & Grape Stomp - St. Augustine	121
WaZoo - Tampa	121

September

Festival - City	Page
Taste of Clearwater - Clearwater	144
Florida Barbecue Association Funcook - Crystal River	72
Taste of Weston - Fort Lauderdale	143
Q-Fest BBQ & Music Festival - Grant	72
Hollywood Beach Clambake - Hollywood	30
'I Like It Hot!' Festival & Barbecue - Largo	131
Florida Cracker Oyster Festival - Orlando	32
Fall Seafood and Pirate Fest - Panama City	31
Emerald Coast Brew Fest & Beach Party - Pensacola	122
Pensacola Seafood Festival - Pensacola	32
Seafood & Mini Wine Fest - Sandestin	29
Sun-N-Fun RV Resort Chili Cookoff - Sarasota	71
Sebastian Clambake Lagoon Festival - Sebastian	30

October

Festival - City	Page
Belleview Chili Cook-off - Belleview	76
Hunsader Farms Pumpkin Festival - Bradenton	106
Hernando County BBQ & Rodeo Festival - Brooksville	74

Food Fest! Your Complete Guide to Florida's Food Festivals

Festival - City	Page
Cedar Key Seafood Festival - Cedar Key	36
Frenchy's Stone Crab Festival - Clearwater Beach	38
Chocolate Festival - Coral Gables	132
Great Bowls of Fire Chili Cookoff - De Land	77
Destin Seafood Festival - Destin	33
Hernando Beach Seafood Festival - Hernando Beach	34
Southeast Chili Cookoff - Homosassa	75
Waterfront Chili Cookoff - Homosassa	76
Gabbert Farm Peanut Festival - Jay	105
Leesburg Chili Cook-Off - Leesburg	78
Stone Crab, Seafood, and Wine Festival - Longboat Key	37
John's Pass Seafood Festival - Madeira Beach	39
Minneola Fall Fest BBQ Contest - Minneola	73
Mulberry Fine Swine At The Pit - Mulberry	73
Boggy Bayou Mullet Festival - Niceville	35
Marion County Chili Cook-Off - Ocala	74
Epcot Food and Wine Festival - Orlando	123
Indian Summer Seafood Festival - Panama City Beach	34
Taste of Plant City - Plant City	144
Stone Crab Fest - Summerland Key	37
Taste at Bay Street - Tampa	145
Leepa-Rattner Museum of Art Stone Crab Fest - Tarpon Springs	36
Central Florida Peanut Festival - Williston	104
Hospice Chili Cookoff - Wilton Manors	77

November

Festival - City	Page
Florida Seafood Festival - Apalachicola	39
Taste of Manatee - Bradenton	146
Dunedin Wines the Blues - Dunedin	125
Fort Myers Taste of the Town - Fort Myers	148
City of Sebastian Clambake	50

Festival - City	Page
First Coast Ham Jam - Green Cove Springs	79
Taste of Gulfport - Gulfport	146
Hudson Seafest - Hudson	41
Jensen Beach Pineapple Festival - Jensen Beach	96
Palm Beach County Firefighters/Paramedics M.D.A. Chili Cookoff - Lake Worth	78
Land O' Lakes Flapjack Festival - Land O Lakes	132
Fine Wine & Food Festival - Oldsmar	123
Orlando Beer Festival - Orlando	126
Plant City Pig Jam - Plant City	80
Ruskin Seafood Festival - Ruskin	40
Safety Harbor Wine Festival - Safety Harbor	125
Ribfest - St. Petersburg	79
Tallahassee Wine and Food Festival - Tallahassee	124
Zoofari - Tampa	147

December

Festival - City	Page
Death By Chocolate - Largo	133
Cheesecake Challenge - St. Augustine	134
Beefcember Fest - Starke	81

C Alphabetical Listing

Appendix C lists each festival in alphabetical order. The city where the festival is held is indicated next to the event name.

Alphabetical Listing

Festival - City	Page
99.9 Kiss Country Regional Chili Cookoff - Pembroke Pines	48
A Taste of St. Augustine - St. Augustine	138
A Taste of the Coast An Artful Affair - Port Saint Joe	138
An Evening with EPIC Chefs - St. Augustine	130
Arcadia Watermelon Festival - Arcadia	89
Astor Chamber Of Commerce Chili Cook-off - Astor	58
Backyard BBQ Blast - Jacksonville	62
Battle of the Badges - Largo	68
BBQfest - Tampa	70
Beefcember Fest - Starke	81
Belleview Chili Cook-off - Belleview	76
Bern's Winefest - Tampa	116
Beulah Sausage Festival - Pensacola	61
Biltmore International Food & Wine Weekend - Coral Gables	117
Bluegrass & BBQ Festival - Auburndale	60
Boca Bacchanal Winefest - Boca Raton	112
Boggy Barbecue Cookoff - Niceville	66
Boggy Bayou Mullet Festival - Niceville	35
Bostwick Blueberry Festival - Bostwick	93
Bradford County Strawberry Festival - Starke	88
Buckhead Ridge Catfish Festival - Buckhead Ridge	8
Cactus Jack's Chili Cookoff - Salt Springs	59
Cajun Blues Crawfish Festival - Palm Beach	18
Cajun Cafe on the Bayou Crawfish Festival - Pinellas Park	20
Cajun Zydeco Crawfish Festival - St. Petersburg	13
Cedar Key Seafood Festival - Cedar Key	36
Celebrate Bonita District Chili Cookoff - Bonita Springs	66
Central Florida BBQ Festival - Sebring	44
Central Florida Peanut Festival - Williston	104
Cheesecake Challenge - St. Augustine	134
Chiefland Watermelon Festival - Chiefland	90

C - Alphabetical Listing

Festival - City	Page
Chili Blaze - Pinellas Park	62
Chili in the Village Regional Cookoff - Pinecrest	54
Chocolate Festival - Coral Gables	132
Clamerica Celebration - Cedar Key	28
Coral Gables Wine & Food Festival - Coral Gables	114
Cortez Commercial Fishing Festival - Cortez	11
Cotee River Seafood Festival and Boat Show - New Port Richey	26
Daytona Beach Bayou Boil - Daytona Beach	26
Death By Chocolate - Largo	133
DeLand Wild Game Feast - De Land	68
Delray Beach Garlic Fest - Delray Beach	100
Denning's Lounge Chili Cookoff - Tampa	63
DeSoto County Watermelon Festival - Arcadia	89
Destin Seafood Festival - Destin	33
'Do It At The Line' Super Chili Bowl Cookoff - Pensacola	51
Dunedin Wines the Blues - Dunedin	125
Einstein on Wine - Tampa	108
Emerald Coast Brew Fest & Beach Party - Pensacola	122
Englewood Beach / Burr Smidt Memorial Chili Cookoff - Englewood	63
Epcot Food and Wine Festival - Orlando	123
Estero High Key Club Chili Cookoff - Estero	55
Everglades Seafood Festival - Everglades	10
Fall Seafood and Pirate Fest - Panama City	31
Fellsmere Frog Leg Festival - Fellsmere	46
Fine Wine & Food Festival - Oldsmar	123
Firefight at Spanish Springs - The Villages	52
First Coast Ham Jam - Green Cove Springs	79
Flan Fest - Tampa	129
Floral City Strawberry Festival - Floral City	87
Florida Barbecue Association Funcook - Crystal River	72
Florida Brewers Guild BeerFest - Tampa	111

Festival - City	Page
Florida Citrus Festival - Winter Haven	84
Florida Cracker Oyster Festival - Orlando	32
Florida Keys Regional Cookoff - Key Largo	55
Florida Keys Seafood Festival - Key West	9
Florida Keys Tropical Fruit Fiesta - Key West	95
Florida Seafood Festival - Apalachicola	39
Florida Strawberry Festival - Plant City	86
Florida Sunshine Pod Cookoff - Englewood	64
Florida Wine Festival - Tallahassee	113
Florida Winefest & Auction - Sarasota	116
Folio Weekly Beer & Music Festival - Jacksonville	120
Fort Myers Beach Shrimp Festival - Fort Myers Beach	14
Fort Myers Taste Of The Beach - Fort Myers Beach	142
Fort Myers Taste of the Town - Fort Myers	148
Frenchy's Stone Crab Festival - Clearwater Beach	38
Gabbert Farm Peanut Festival - Jay	105
Gavel & Grapes Festival - Tarpon Springs	120
Goodland Mullet Festival - Marco Island	8
Grant Seafood Festival - Grant	11
Great American Pie Festival - Orlando	129
Great Atlantic Seafood Festival - Jacksonville	16
Great Bowls of Fire Chili Cookoff - De Land	77
Great Northwest Rib & Family Fest - Tampa	50
Great Southern Gumbo Cook-off - Sandestin	45
Grillin & Chillin on Main Wauchula - Wauchula	50
Gulf Coast Regional Chili Cookoff - Eastpoint	56
Gulf County Scallop Festival - Port Saint Joe	29
Harbor Sounds Seafood & Music Festival - Safety Harbor	12
Hernando Beach Seafood Festival - Hernando Beach	34
Hernando County BBQ & Rodeo Festival - Brooksville	74
Hog Wild and Pig Crazy Barbecue Cook-off - Lake City	64
Hollywood Beach Clambake - Hollywood	30
Honey Festival - La Belle	128

C - Alphabetical Listing

Festival - City	Page
Hospice Chili Cookoff - Wilton Manors	77
Hudson Seafest - Hudson	41
Hunsader Farms Pumpkin Festival - Bradenton	106
'I Like It Hot!' Festival & Barbecue - Largo	131
Indian River County Firefighters' Chili Cookoff - Vero Beach	70
Indian Summer Seafood Festival - Panama City Beach	34
International Mango Festival - Coral Gables	94
Isle Of Eight Flags Shrimp Festival - Fernandina Beach	24
Jefferson County Watermelon Festival - Monticello	92
Jensen Beach Pineapple Festival - Jensen Beach	96
Jim's Chili Cookoff - St. Petersburg	45
John's Pass Seafood Festival - Madeira Beach	39
Jumbalaya Jam - Melbourne	10
Key West Food and Wine Festival - Key West	119
Kumquat Festival - Dade City	84
Lakeland Pig Festival - Lakeland	48
Lakeridge Winefest - Clermont	109
Land O' Lakes Flapjack Festival - Land O Lakes	132
Las Olas Wine and Food Festival - Fort Lauderdale	118
Leepa-Rattner Museum of Art Stone Crab Fest - Tarpon Springs	36
Leesburg Chili Cook-Off - Leesburg	78
'Make it Mild or Make it Wild' Chili Cook-off - Jacksonville	65
Mangomania Tropical Fruit Fair - Pine Island	96
Marathon Seafood Festival - Marathon	16
Marion County Chili Cook-Off - Ocala	74
Miami Wine and Food Festival - Miami	112
Minneola Fall Fest BBQ Contest - Minneola	73
Mulberry Fine Swine At The Pit - Mulberry	73
Naples Country Jam Chili Cookoff - Naples	60
Naples Winter Wine Festival - Naples	108
National Shrimp and Oyster Festival - Panama City	21
New Times Beerfest - Fort Lauderdale	114

179

Festival - City	Page
Newberry Watermelon Festival - Newberry	90
Northeast Florida Blueberries & Barbecue Festival - Callahan	92
Orlando Beer Festival - Orlando	126
Palatka Blue Crab Festival - Palatka	27
Palm Beach County Firefighters/Paramedics M.D.A. Chili Cookoff - Lake Worth	78
Palm Beach Seafood Festival - Palm Beach	15
Panacea Blue Crab Festival - Panacea	25
Panhandle Watermelon Festival - Chipley	94
Pensacola Crawfish Creole Fiesta - Pensacola	24
Pensacola Seafood Festival - Pensacola	32
Pig on the Pond - Clermont	57
Placida Rotary Seafood Festival - Placida	17
Plant City Arts Council Chili Cookoff - Plant City	54
Plant City Pig Jam - Plant City	80
Police, Firefighter, & EMS Chili Cook Off - Winter Haven	49
Pompano Beach Seafood Festival - Pompano Beach	23
Q-Fest BBQ & Music Festival - Grant	72
Rajuncajun Crawfish Festival - Orlando	21
Rhythm and Ribs Festival - St. Augustine	67
Ribfest - St. Petersburg	79
Ruskin Seafood Festival - Ruskin	40
Ruskin Tomato Festival - Ruskin	102
Safety Harbor Wine Festival - Safety Harbor	125
San Sebastian Harvest Festival & Grape Stomp - St. Augustine	121
San Sebastian Winefest - St. Augustine	110
Sandestin Wine Festival - Sandestin	115
Seafood & Mini Wine Fest - Sandestin	29
Sebastian Clambake Lagoon Festival - Sebastian	30
Shores Wine and Food Festival - Daytona Beach	118
Shrimp Fest - Ponce Inlet	22
'Smoke on the Water' BBQ - Winter Haven	53
Smoke 'n Blues BBQ - St. Cloud	69

C - Alphabetical Listing

Festival - City	Page
Sour Orange Festival - Lakeport	85
South Beach Wine and Food Festival - Miami	110
Southeast Chili Cookoff - Homosassa	75
Speckled Perch Festival - Okeechobee	14
Spring Fish Fry - Leesburg	20
Spring Jubilee Chili Cook-off - Riverview	67
St. Augustine Lions Seafood Festival - St. Augustine	18
St. Johns River Catfish Festival - Crescent City	19
Stone Crab Fest - Summerland Key	37
Stone Crab, Seafood, and Wine Festival - Longboat Key	37
Sugar Festival - Clewiston	101
Sun-N-Fun RV Resort Chili Cookoff - Sarasota	71
Suncoast Chili Cookoff - Tarpon Springs	47
Sunshine Regional Chili Cook-Off - Kissimmee	46
Swamp Cabbage Festival - La Belle	100
Sweet Corn Fiesta - West Palm Beach	102
Tallahassee Wine and Food Festival - Tallahassee	124
Taste at Bay Street - Tampa	145
Taste of Boynton - Boynton Beach	141
Taste of Chocolate Festival - Plant City	128
Taste of Clearwater - Clearwater	144
Taste of Collier - Naples	140
Taste of Gulfport - Gulfport	146
Taste of Key West - Key West	137
Taste of Manatee - Bradenton	146
Taste of Mount Dora - Mount Dora	140
Taste of Pine Island - Pine Island	136
Taste of Pinellas - St. Petersburg	142
Taste of Plant City - Plant City	144
Taste of the Beach (Lauderdale-By-The-Sea) - Lauderdale-By-The-Sea	136
Taste of the Islands - Sanibel	139
Taste of Weston - Fort Lauderdale	143

Food Fest! Your Complete Guide to Florida's Food Festivals

Festival - City	*Page*
The Big Squeeze - Palm Bay	88
Titusville Sunrise Rotary Club Chili Cookoff - Titusville	52
Top Of The Lake BBQ Affair - Okeechobee	56
Tupelo Honey Festival - Wewahitchka	130
Waterfront Chili Cookoff - Homosassa	76
WaZoo - Tampa	121
Wellborn Blueberry Festival - Wellborn	91
Windsor Zucchini Festival - Gainesville	103
Zellwood Sweet Corn Festival - Zellwood	104
Zoofari - Tampa	147

D Bonus Recipes

Appendix D contains some recipes to temp your tastebuds. Don't be afraid to experiment with different variations of them—that's how recipes get created in the first place!

Kumquat Refrigerator Pie

1 baked pie crust, 9"
1 (8 oz.) Cool Whip whipped topping
2/3 cup pureed Kumquats
1 can condensed milk
1/2 cup lemon juice

Beat condensed milk and whipped topping. Add lemon juice and beat until thickened. Add pureed kumquats, pour in pie shell and chill in refrigerator for several hours.

Recipe courtesy of Rosemary Gude.

For additional delicious kumquat recipes, visit the Kumquat Growers Inc.'s website at http://www.kumquatgrowers.com

Joan's Famous Black Bean & Veggie Chili

1/2 lb. lean ground beef or ground turkey - browned, crumbled, drained
1 can black beans - rinsed and drained
3 medium carrots - sliced
1 bell pepper - diced (green, red, or yellow – you decide)
1 medium onion
1/2 jar (8 oz.) of salsa (mild, medium, or hot – again, you decide)
2 cans (16 oz.) tomato sauce (more or less, depending on how soupy you want it. Add the tomato sauce last so you can adjust to your liking.)
1 package of chili seasoning mix

Add all ingredients to a 4-quart crock pot. Let cook on High for 5-6 hours, or on Low for around 12 hours, or until the veggies are the consistency you like.

Notes:
  • If you like it spicier, add some hot sauce. I usually just add it to my own bowl later since not everyone likes it with as much kick as I do (go figure!).
  • You can double the recipe if you have a large crockpot. Leftovers taste even better the second day and freeze well.

Index

A

agriculture exhibits 86
airplanes 17
amusement rides 97, 104
animal world 85
antiques 2, 24, 28, 85, 87, 90, 94, 103, 105, 146
Arts
  art auction 147
  artists 111, 139
  Art Safari 147
  art show 101
  authors 139
  caricature artist 144
  fine arts 24, 28, 86
  paintings 139
  photography 84, 139
  prints 139
arts and crafts 10, 11, 12, 13, 15, 16, 17, 18, 19, 21, 22, 23, 24, 25, 26, 28, 29, 31, 32, 34, 35, 36, 40, 41, 46, 47, 50, 51, 58, 61, 70, 72, 79, 88, 91, 92, 93, 94, 96, 97, 101, 103, 104, 105, 109, 121, 125, 131, 133, 147
auction 57, 65, 89, 91, 95, 96, 108, 109, 112, 113, 116, 117, 119, 121, 125, 130, 137, 142, 147

B

balloon rides 18
barnyard playground 106
Beach Party 122
bike show 62
boat show 17, 30, 40
boat tours 26, 28
bounce house 69, 71
buffalo farm 61

C

cane grinding 101
carnival 41, 50, 58, 61, 65, 74, 84, 87, 88, 90, 105
carousel 102
car show 15, 19, 27, 68, 70, 71, 80, 85, 87, 88, 94, 101, 121, 146
celebrity chefs 108, 117, 142
chainsaw sculpting 106
children's activities 2, 11, 12, 15, 21, 23, 24, 25, 26, 27, 29, 31, 35, 39, 40, 45, 48, 51, 54, 65, 67, 69, 75, 80, 85, 87, 88, 91, 93, 94, 95, 96, 97, 100, 103, 106, 129, 130, 138, 142
circus tent 106
Civil War re-enactors 51
clogging 61, 106
clowns 17, 18, 23, 35, 52, 93, 97
Competitions
  bartender contest 27
  Battle of the Bars 119
  Beer Olympics 123
  best booth 44, 52, 59
  bubble gum 105
  children's costume contests 31
  chili dog eating 62
  corn eating 102, 104
  corn shucking 104
  crab races 17, 23
  dueling banjos 61
  flan eating 129
  flapjack eating 133
  Garlic Chef 100
  grapefruit packing 84
  grape stomping 122, 125
  hay bale decorating 84
  hog calling 44, 90
  home grown fruit 96
  hot-wing eating 71
  hot dog eating 71
  ice-carving 140

mango cook-off 95
Mr. and Mrs. Chili Pepper 57
old-fashioned bathing suit 102
oyster eating 40
oyster shucking 40
pepper eating 131
pet dress-up 105
photography 84
pie-eating 85
pig chase 105
quilt challenge 85
raft races 30
recipe contest 85
seed-spitting 89, 90, 91
shortcake eating 86
Waiter/Waitress 140, 143
watermelon eating 90
watermelon roll 90
window decorating 85
zucchini carving 103
Contests. *See* Competitions
cooking/ culinary demonstrations 38, 48, 110, 111, 123, 130
  cooking classes 119
  cooking session 113
  cooking shows 88
  cooking theater 142
Cookoffs
  barbecue cook-off 44, 51, 56, 63, 64, 66, 81, 93, 152, 166, 174, 176
  blueberry bake-off 94
  blueberry cookoff 93
  cake competition 75
  children's pie making 130
  chili cook-off 45, 46, 47, 48, 49, 51, 52, 54, 55, 56, 59, 60, 62, 63, 64, 65, 66, 68, 70, 71, 74, 75, 76, 77, 78, 152, 155, 156, 157, 164, 165, 166, 168, 169, 170, 171, 174, 175, 176, 177, 178, 179, 180

dessert bake-off 58
dessert contest 102
flan contest 129
hot sauce 131
pie/cake baking 90
recipe contest 85
salsa 46, 55
seafood chowder 136
zucchini cooking contest 103
Crafters. *See* Arts and crafts

D

dance/dancing 8, 13, 14, 21, 38, 59, 65, 92, 94, 116, 121, 124, 129, 142

E

environmental exhibits 11

F

face painting 17, 23, 71, 131
farmers market 88
farming equipment 101, 105
fashion show 16
fireworks 21, 24, 25, 28, 68, 142
flea market 17, 59, 61
floats 87
Food
  alligator 10, 12, 13, 17, 19, 35, 47
  barbecue 3, 12, 43, 44, 48, 51, 53, 54, 56, 57, 58, 60, 61, 62, 63, 64, 66, 67, 69, 70, 72, 73, 74, 79, 80, 81, 92, 93, 105, 106, 131
  blueberries 91, 92, 93
  catfish 8, 9, 10, 19, 33
  cheesecake 134
  chili 45, 46, 47, 48, 49, 51, 52, 54, 55, 56, 57, 58, 59, 60, 62, 63, 64, 65, 66, 67, 68, 69, 70, 71, 72, 74, 75, 76, 77, 78, 79

Index

chocolate 128, 132, 133
chowder 9, 10, 28, 30, 31, 136
citrus 84
clams 12, 17, 28, 30, 31
conch 9, 12
corn, sweet 102, 104, 106
crab 9, 12, 17, 23, 25, 27, 36, 37, 38, 39, 153, 155, 156, 160, 168, 170, 176, 177, 178, 179
crawfish 13, 18, 19, 20, 21, 22, 24, 25, 27, 32
flan 129
flapjacks. See pancakes
frog legs 10, 12, 46, 47
fruit, tropical 95, 96
garlic 100
garlic ice cream 100
grapefruit 84
grouper 17, 39, 41
gumbo 13, 17, 19, 21, 28, 45
Heart of Palm 101
honey 128, 130, 131
jambalaya 12, 13, 21, 25
kumquat 84
kumquat pie 84
lobster 9, 17
mango 94, 95, 96
mullet 8, 17, 25, 32, 35
orange 85
oysters 12, 17, 20, 21, 32, 33, 40, 57
pancakes 92, 93, 132, 133
peanut 104, 105
pie buffet 129, 130
pineapple 96, 97
pumpkin 106
pumpkin pie 106
sausage 17, 61
scallops 12, 29
shrimp 12, 14, 17, 21, 22, 23, 24, 39
stone crab 9, 10, 36, 37, 38

strawberry 86, 87, 88
sugar 101
swamp cabbage 19, 100
tomato 102, 103
watermelon 89, 90, 91, 92, 94
zucchini 103
zucchini ice cream 103
fun zone 23, 24, 26

G

Garlic University 100
- *Great for Kids!* 10, 11, 12, 13, 14, 15, 16, 17, 18, 19, 21, 22, 23, 24, 25, 26, 27, 28, 29, 30, 31, 33, 34, 35, 36, 39, 40, 41, 44, 45, 46, 48, 50, 53, 57, 61, 64, 65, 67, 68, 69, 70, 72, 74, 76, 79, 80, 84, 86, 87, 88, 89, 90, 92, 93, 94, 95, 96, 100, 101, 102, 103, 104, 105, 106, 129, 130, 132, 138, 142, 144, 145, 146, 148
gristmill 105

H

Harley Davidson show 80
hay rides 105, 106
horseback riding 131
horse show 90
horticulture exhibits 86
hot pepper plants 131
hot rod show 27

K

Kid's activities. *See* Children's activities

L

livestock 74, 84, 86

M

magician 18, 93, 144
marching bands 87

189

marine equipment 17
midway 15, 47, 50, 58, 68, 87, 133
monster truck show, 93
moonwalk 105, 138
motorcycle show 47, 70
musical entertainment 1, 9, 10, 11,
    12, 13, 15, 16, 17, 18, 19,
    21, 22, 23, 24, 25, 26, 28,
    29, 31, 35, 36, 37, 38, 39,
    41, 45, 46, 49, 51, 54, 55,
    56, 59, 61, 62, 63, 69, 70,
    71, 72, 74, 75, 76, 77, 85,
    87, 88, 89, 96, 97, 102, 103,
    104, 105, 106, 109, 111,
    113, 115, 118, 119, 120,
    122, 124, 126, 134, 136,
    138, 139, 143, 145, 147, 148
  bands 27, 63, 65, 115, 123, 140
  Bluegrass 18, 61
  Blues 11, 12, 18, 70, 125
  Cajun 11, 21, 22, 27
  concerts 34, 79, 80, 86, 94, 142
  Country 49, 61, 70, 74, 79
  dueling banjos 61
  Jazz 15, 111, 144
  Oldies 12
  Reggae 15
  Rock 12, 15
  Swamp Pop 13

P

pageant 24, 35, 84, 85, 87, 90, 92,
    103
parade 14, 15, 19, 24, 25, 28, 40,
    56, 84, 85, 90, 91, 92, 94,
    101, 105, 133
petting zoo 94, 106
pirates 24, 31
plant clinic 96
ponies 35, 105, 106

Q

Queens 2, 8, 14, 40, 87, 89, 91,
    101, 103, 105
quilt exhibition 101

R

raffle 16, 63, 65, 76, 77, 143, 144

S

seaplane rides 54
slide 65, 69, 101
Sporting events
  10K run 123
  5K run 16, 19, 57, 72, 85, 90
  bass tournament 101
  beach volleyball tournament 30
  bike ride 63
  cross country run 35
  fishing tournament 41, 63
  fun run 103
  golf tournament 90, 113, 117
  horseshoe tournament 101
  paintball 63
  rock-climbing wall 101, 105
  rodeo 14, 15, 74, 92, 101
  sailboat races 41
  softball tournament 92
street entertainment 97

T

tractor pull 105
tractor show 103

W

Wine events
  food and wine pairing 110, 119
  seminars 110, 112, 116, 117, 119,
    123
  vintner dinners 108, 112
  wine auction 108, 116
  wine garden 100, 121
  winemaker dinners 117
  wine tasting 29, 70, 110, 111,
    112, 113, 116, 119, 122,
    124, 125 130, 142, 143

About the Author

Joan Steinbacher is a writer, information technology professional, and avid food fest fanatic. She has lived on the Gulf Coast and enjoyed Florida's food festivals for over fifteen years. When not writing, she enjoys kayaking and other outdoor activities.

www.BeeCliffPress.com

How To Order

Online Orders: Visit our website at http://www.FoodFestGuide.com

Postal Orders: Mail completed order form with payment (check, money order, or credit card number) to Bee Cliff Press, P.O. Box 8598, Seminole, FL 33775.

Fax Orders: Fax completed order form to 800-930-4731 (toll-free).

Telephone Orders: Call 800-930-4731 (toll-free).

Title	Quantity	Total Dollars
Food Fest! Your Complete Guide to Florida's Food Festivals, $14.95		
Subtotal (in dollars)		
Florida residents, please add applicable state and local sales tax.		
Shipping (add $3.99 for 1-2 books, and $1.00 for each additional book.)		
TOTAL AMOUNT		

My check or money order is enclosed, payable to "Bee Cliff Press"
   - OR -

Please charge my Visa / MasterCard (circle one)
    Name on Credit Card _____
    Card # _____
    Exp. Date (month and year) _____
    Card Verification Number (3-digit code on back of card) _____
    Signature _____

Shipping Address:
    Name _____
    Address _____
    City / State / Zip _____
    Phone _____ E-mail _____

Payment must accompany orders. Please allow 3 weeks for delivery.
Questions? Send an e-mail to info@BeeCliffPress.com

Henscratch Farms - Any Annual Grape Stomp & Music Fest
www.henscratchfarms.com
863-699-2060